DESIGN FOR COMPOSITION

INSPIRATION FOR CREATIVE VISUAL AND MULTIMODAL PROJECTS

D1601820

SOHUI LEE
RUSSELL CARPENTER

Parlor Press
Anderson, South Carolina
www.parlorpress.com

Parlor Press LLC, Anderson, South Carolina, USA
© 2023 by Parlor Press
All rights reserved.
Printed in the United States of America on acid-free paper.

S A N: 2 5 4 - 8 8 7 9

Library of Congress Cataloging-in-Publication Data on File

978-1-64317-306-1 (paperback)
978-1-64317-307-8 (pdf)
978-1-64317-308-5 (epub)

1 2 3 4 5

Interior Design: Lindsay Scott

Parlor Press, LLC is an independent publisher of scholarly and trade titles in print and multimedia formats. This book is available in paper and ebook formats from Parlor Press on the World Wide Web at https://parlorpress.com or through online and brick-and-mortar bookstores. For submission information or to find out about Parlor Press publications, write to Parlor Press, 3015 Brackenberry Drive, Anderson, South Carolina, 29621, or email editor@parlorpress.com.

DESIGN FOR COMPOSITION

CHAPTER OVERVIEW

CHAPTER	LEARNING OUTCOMES
Chapter 1 Visualizing and Feeling Observation: Found Creativity Through Elements of Art	• **Discover** how elements of art (line, color, shape, texture, and space) may be used in a creative way for a range of day-to-day purposes. • **Analyze** and compare creative art elements in visual or tactile modalities. • **Reflect** on each of the creative objects you've chosen by explaining why it is "creative." • **Propose** a definition of creativity based on your observations and interactions with art elements.
Chapter 2 Visualizing Observation: Understanding Design Principles through Vintage Ads and Posters	• **Discover** how design principles (unity, balance, focalization, and repetition) may be used creatively in print advertisements for a range of meaning/messages. • **Analyze and compare** one design principle employed in at least five print ads (analyzing three print ads in detail). • **Reflect** on three of the print ads by explaining how a visual design principle conveys the message creatively. • **Reflect** on what you learned from others. How do their analyses of design principles differ from yours?
Chapter 3 Feeling Observation: Touch Test in Product Design	• **Discover** how designing for touch (texture, shape, mass) may be used creatively to convey a range of meaning/messages. • **Analyze** one perfume or cologne bottle in terms of texture, shape, or mass to determine 1) the target audience; and 2) the message conveyed about the product. • **Reflect** on whether the perfume or cologne matches your analysis by touch alone. What is touch adding to your understanding.
Chapter 4 Speaking Application: Vocal Expression	• **Explore** how voice carries distinct personality profiles or mood attributes. • **Apply** vocalics strategy from one genre (creative work) to another (academic essay). • **Reflect** on your choices in vocalics subject and application
Chapter 5 Interacting Application: Thinking/Rethinking App Icons for an Everyday Activity	• **Distill** an everyday activity to an essential concept, develop key word(s). • **Think/rethink** multiple versions of a concept with prototypes that modify or combine noun project icons and play with color. • **Learn** to use the Picture Format Tool creatively. • **Share** your app design to see who can guess the concept.

CHAPTER	LEARNING OUTCOMES
Chapter 6 Touching Evaluation: Creativity in Clothing and Texture	• **Learn** about basic categories of visual and tactile texture in fabric. • **Explore** how visual and tactile textures may communicate. • **Generate** a rubric of the creative use of texture. • **Apply** the rubric to a creative item of clothing.
Chapter 7 Speaking and Writing Application: Ventriloquy and Rhetorical Devices	• **Understand and identify** the effect of common rhetorical devices. • **Identify** specific rhetorical devices in a famous speech. • **Apply** rhetorical devices creatively in your ventriloquy. • **Reflect** on your choices (and the choices of others).
Chapter 8 Performing Application: Instrumental Theme Songs for the News	• **Explore** how sound creates emotion, energy, interest, and empathy in its listeners and audience members. • **Analyze** applications and uses of sounds in broadcasting. • **Create** a soundtrack for a news broadcast. • **Reflect** on the decisions you made in selecting sounds.
Chapter 9 Composing Production: Making Your Own Portmanteau	• **Apply** divergent thinking by generating many words associated with a particular idea. • **Combine** two or more syllables/sounds from two words to generate a new word. • **Reflect** on your and others' choices by sharing.
Chapter 10 Seeing Production: Album Art and Discovering Typography	• **Explore** how typefaces carry personality profiles or attributes. • **Translate** concepts from one modality (sound) to another (visual). • **Create** an album cover with typeface, layout, and color. • **Reflect** on your creative choices in typeface and design.
Chapter 11 Performing Production: Contact [Object] Improvisation	• **Explore and create** new body movement possibilities. • **Increase** awareness of your own physicality and movement. • **Reflect** on your creative movements and your own body voice, **connect** with oral communication.

CONTENTS

PREFACE FOR STUDENTS

Every day, we are constantly processing and receiving messages that are communicated to us through all our senses and the environment: words, images, shapes, textures, sound, and spaces. If, in the last century, *literacy* was primarily defined by our ability to read (consume writing) and write (produce writing), we now live in the century when people are increasingly expected to communicate and critically understand written and non-written forms of communication, or what we call modalities. In social media, platforms have moved beyond SMS and text messages to encourage users to produce and share visuals and videos. Smart watches not only provide text and visual content but also haptic feedback through vibrations and tactile keys. Some consider haptic feedback one of the most exciting new sensory environments yet to be explored as companies develop virtual reality applications. In our technologically-enhanced, internet-connected, socially-mediated world, our ability to be "literate" has been redefined; and just as strong skills in writing require intentional learning, peoples' skills in communicating across modalities also need to be intentionally learned and honed.

Although technologies will change, our need and ability to communicate through different modalities will only increase. One of the goal of this book is to increase your awareness of the range of ways communication happens, the context in which it happens, and solve communication problems by thinking creatively. For instance, you will learn through creativity projects how to intentionally practice divergent thinking (generate free flow of ideas beyond the first few thoughts that come to mind) and how to practice convergent thinking (systematically narrowing ideas to solutions that are more likely to address a specific problem). In addition, many of the creative projects, such as making album art or creating a portmanteau word, are designed to help you become more attuned to specific skill areas across a variety of text-based, visual, oral, and even physical modalities. You will also experiment with specific technological applications—tools that allow you to intentionally consider creativity's role in the design and composition process—pushing boundaries of your knowledge and depth of experience—to explore fresh approaches.

Through all this, the projects are intentionally hands-on, focusing on application or "doing," while also encouraging you to reflect on the process of creativity and creation. You'll find that even the challenge of working through a creative design project helps you become more aware, intentional, and critical communicators, thinkers, and learners. Along the way, you'll observe *how* you complete the steps of the project (components that are often overlooked in favor of a final, finished, or correct product). As you navigate its chapters and projects, *Design for Composition* will encourage you to think about creative processes in communication with the goal of increasing awareness of what you're doing along the way. Broken down into smaller steps, the projects will help you develop a conscious understanding of how creativity may be applied in composition.

ACKNOWLEDGMENTS

We would like to acknowledge the many people who believed in this project and express our appreciation for their commitment to supporting us along the way. *Design for Composition* is inspired by many conversations about the role of creativity in multimodal composing, from classrooms to multiliteracy centers, and more broadly learning spaces. In particular, we would like to gratefully acknowledge the support of Dave Blakesley for his enthusiasm for this project and thoughtful feedback for the book. We are also thankful to Lindsay Scott for designing a layout that helps students appreciate the content we created!

Sohui would like to thank the Program in Writing and Rhetoric at Stanford University, for permitting a creative pedagogical environment where parts of this project were originally conceived and explored in classrooms. She is also grateful for the support of many colleagues at CSU Channel Islands, but particularly Dr. Ekin Pehlivan, whose encouragement and conversations inspired her to believe that a textbook like *Design for Composition* would be useful, not only in composition instruction but in other fields like business where creative thinking is crucial for effective communication. Sohui also wants to acknowledge the contribution of the peer tutors in the Writing & Multiliteracy Center at CSU Channel Islands. They were asked to conduct some of the creativity challenges and provided helpful feedback. Finally, Sohui is ever thankful to James, Iain, and Auden for being patient when she worked some weekends.

Russell would like to express gratitude to Eastern Kentucky University for supporting the range of innovative and creative initiatives that inspired much of this project. He acknowledges the Noel Studio for Academic Creativity for inspiring the creative projects featured here. The students and consultants pushed boundaries in creative thinking that continue to challenge us to explore new approaches to design.

0 INTRODUCTION
DESIGN FOR
COMPOSITION

PURPOSE

What is rhetoric in the twenty-first century? What does it mean for our students to be "literate" in the age of digital media? In a landmark article written early in this century, Pamela Takayoshi and Cynthia L. Selfe (2007) surmised that twenty-first century literacy would need to include proficiency in multiliteracies if students were to be prepared for whatever profession they hope to enter—from being a primary school educator to an engineer; from working as a marketer to presenting data as a researcher. Specifically, Takayoshi and Selfe established an early argument for the importance of teaching students how to apply visual, verbal, vocal, and multimodal rhetoric. Indeed, more than a decade later, the National Association of Colleges and Employers (NACE) updated their description of communication competency for career readiness; expectations in basic competencies in communication expanded from verbal and written language skills to include "nonverbal/body language [and] abilities." One of the major aims of this workbook is to provide activity projects that help students explore skills across a fuller range of communication modalities through creative thinking processes.

Design for Composition offers an assortment of projects ranging in modes as well as stages of composition process(es) and creativity objectives. These options allow for instructors to assign projects based on the goals of their visual, oral, or multimedia-focused composition courses or writing/multiliteracy centers. Moreover, *Design for Composition* is unique in being the only composition workbook that centrally integrates creativity skills and ways of creative thinking. Creativity is situational and iterative, and creative approaches help students engage with both the relational constraints and inventive experimentation to compose effective multimodal messages. For instance, James Purdy (2014) highlights the way prototyping in design thinking (a version of creative thinking) can reinvigorate writing practices. Creativity pushes students to think more critically about composition strategies by employing new technologies or playing in new ways with familiar ones. Drawing from scholarship in creativity, composition, and pedagogy, *Design for Composition* engages students in the composition process that is situated in creative cognitive stages.

This workbook is organized into chapters on creative projects that can be used in classrooms across a range of course deliveries, including those in hybrid or flexible formats, with a mix of high- and low-tech multimodal projects that can be integrated into online or in-person classrooms. Each chapter includes materials that can be used for in-person or online activities to promote creativity in the composing process across a variety of contexts. Moreover, the expected duration of these creative projects range from one hour assignments to multi-day projects. Emphasizing the appreciation of process rather than product, *Design for Composition's* hands-on projects may be considered a kind of "construction site," turning exploration, questions, and even frustrations into valuable experiences that focus on the connections among creativity, design, and rhetoric (Anderson 2008).

Creative projects include learning objectives that help students explore—and re-explore—how argument informs design in different forms of communication modes. In addition, the workbook format allows instructors to choose from among a range of activities for use in a variety of learning contexts. Unique features include activities supported by examples, free tools for exploring creative design activities, Creativity Doing (an overview of the creative project and directions), and Creativity Reflecting (guided prompts for thinking deeply about creative projects), and modular creative projects.

PEDAGOGY

Why is multimodal communication important?

Speaking to TESOL professionals, a renowned semiotics scholar announced his intent to "unsettle" the way teachers focused on teaching written text. Gunther Kress noted,

A revolution in the landscape of communication is changing its configurations fundamentally. . . . A look at a newspaper of 30 or 40 years ago will show at once the characteristics and the extent of that change: The newspapers of, say, 1960 and even of 1970 are covered in print; its successor paper in 2000 is mostly likely to have a lot more space given over to image than to print. (2000, 337)

If Kress were to update his newspaper example for today, he might say that its characteristics would show an even more profound transformation in how we communicate in the twenty-first century: most major newspapers now have a joint print and online presence. In cases like the venerable *Newsweek* magazine, the print publication was discontinued. Newspapers are not only giving more space to images; a quick look at one page of an online newspaper like the *New York Times* reveals that news is hyperlinked to other related news articles, interactive through readers' comments, animated with video clips or infographics, socially mediated through Facebook, Instagam, TikTok, Twitter, WhatApp, LinkedIn, and Reddit, and finally, read on multiple digital platforms from desktops and laptops to tablets and smartphones. The multimodal features of the *New York Times* reaffirm the validity of Kress's assertion that "it is no longer possible to understand language and its uses without understanding the effect of all modes of communication that are copresent in any text" (2000, 337).

Most arguments supporting multiliteracies and multimodal pedagogy today make a point similar to Kress's: the communication practices of our world have changed dramatically, and multimodal literacy is needed to equip students "with the knowledge and skills . . . to access higher education, find employment, and participate in all aspects of contemporary life" (Wolfe and Flewitt 2010). With the technological and social changes that have happened since the beginning of the twenty-first century, communication channels have multiplied in new digital environments that support "cultural and global multicultural ecologies" (Selfe and Selfe 2008, 86). However, multimodality is not only about digital communication. Based on the works of the New London Group, and Kress and van Leeuwen, multimodal literacy theory describes a "communicational landscape" constituting multimodal texts—from gestures we use while talking to public signs to architecture to more obvious technological environments of Power-Point presentations, blogs, and videos (Kress and van Leeuwen 2001, 46). For Kress and van Leeuwen in *Multimodal Discourse*, the multimodal principle takes into account the full range of semiotic modes: "The traditional linguistic account is one in which meaning is made once, so to speak. By contrast, we see the multimodal resources which are available in a culture used to make meanings in any and every sign, at every level, and in any mode" (4).

We revisit Kress and van Leeuwen's broad notion of multimodality because it is the foundation for the principles behind this workbook. We believe that multimodal literacy (the ability to read but also create multimodal messages) should involve the study of expressive possibilities in verbal, visual, tactile, physical, and/or aural modalities. Chapters in this book are designed to help students and others interested in exploring and teaching multimodal communication to critically focus on answering questions such as these:

- How are these modalities designed?
- What are the intended effects on audiences? How do modalities impact the audience's reception of the message differently than other modalities?
- How are students effective in communicating the message or persuading the audience?
- What creative techniques or strategies can be applied when using these modalities?

Why design?

While the study and practice of multimodality grew during the last few decades, design studies have also gained considerable interest in composition, particularly due to the growing interest in visual rhetoric or multimodality. Frank Serafini argued that theoretical tools needed for multimodal pedagogy involve the teaching of visual design (2011). Beyond visual design principles, the process of design thinking has also been brought to the attention of composition scholars. Matthew Newcomb has made a case for "design-orientated" thinking in composition to relate the situational relationships emphasized in design (2012, 596). Design, he argued, is "a rhetorical process" and "is more about thoughts and activities than about products" (584). While Newcomb's proposal to connect design and rhetoric is not the first, his introduction to design thinking is an important next step in expanding students' understanding of the rhetorical nature of design that is helpful for learning multimodality.

Design process makes particular sense when we compare its similarities to the composition process, which remains fundamental to multimodal composition. According to Christine Edwards-Groves, "Creating dynamic multidimensional texts requires understanding the multimodal writing process which enables recursive movement from planning to presenting, from drafting to designing" (2012, 101). The composition stages of planning, drafting, revising, and presenting find a parallel in design, but design's approach brings in an explicit understanding of process-driven thinking. Central to design thinking and strategy is the tenet: "Express. Test. Cycle" (Doorley and Witthoft 2012, 73).

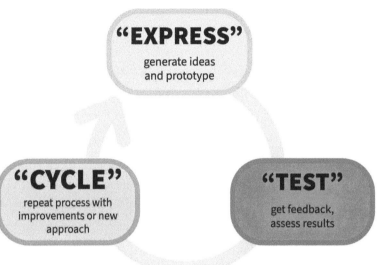

Figure 1: Express-test-cycle stages in design, Doorley and Witthoft 2012.

"Express" refers to the stage in which designers generate creative ideas and build low-tech prototypes. "Test" is the stage when designers look for feedback and reaction, and reflect on the results. And finally "Cycle" is when they repeat the process, modifying the expression or creating a new one and testing it again. David Kelly, founder of Stanford's d.school and IDEO, calls the "express" stage or prototyping phase "enlightened trial and error" (qtd. in Doorley and Witholf 2012, 73, our emphasis), thus pointing to the value of its tentative nature. The equivalent stage in composition might be a combination of "brainstorming" and "drafting"—however, the difference between composition and design lies in the attitude or what Newcomb calls the "frame of mind" in this particular design situation. In design, the Express stage expects no mastery; in fact, it prepares students to anticipate and even desire failure: "A 'failed' or poorly received prototype," write Doorley and Witholf, "that yields big insights can be far more valuable than a 'successful' one that confirms previous thinking" (2012, 73). Regardless of the success of the final product, the real value is in the creative thinking gained from the process.

A valuable design concept is the notion that creativity is learned, not innate—it takes practice and evolves through quick cycles through prototyping practice. Design philosophy teaches students to expect but also desire multiple iterations of prototyping and feedback before a valuable innovative idea emerges. Composition students who approach the "drafting" process of their multimodal project with this frame of mind are asked to think **through** their drafts, rather than **with** their drafts. In other words, approach the draft as a **process of thinking**, rather than only as a means to create a multimedia product. This philosophy of design is also central to this workbook. Many projects involve activities that ask students to "express" and "test" their projects and "cycle" or repeat the process to improve the prototype or make another one. The design approach of creativity heightens metacognition and reflection on multimodal projects, which students will document in their reflection on their activities.

Why creativity?

Derived from the Latin word *invenire* ("to find") and originally discussed in terms of oratorical composition, invention in classical rhetoric is one of the five "canons" of rhetoric, in addition to arrangement, style, memory, and delivery. In fact, Cicero lists invention first in Book One of *De Inventione*: for Cicero, invention, the art of discovering an appropriate topic, was essential for capturing the audience's good will and helping them be disposed to the argument. In modern composition, invention is taught as one of the early critical stages of writing: the stage of brainstorming or discovery during which writers identify topics or ideas on which to write. However, the classic notion of invention, while associated with developing topics, was never specifically isolated to a brainstorming stage in writing. In *De Inventione*, Cicero states that all of argumentation, by its very nature, involves invention and suggests that the principle of invention can be enacted not only in the *exordium* (the address) but also other parts of the argument such as the *narratio* (contextualization of the argument).

From this perspective, invention (idea finding) could happen at any or every stage of the composition process (brainstorming, outlining, drafting, and revising). In this book, we approach invention in communication as part of creativity, the ability to engage problem solving in imaginative ways. Through the works of Flower and Hayes (1977, 1980, 1981), Elbow (1983), and Carey and Flower (1989), creativity was introduced in composition literature as a heuristic through creative thinking studies (Lee and Carpenter 2015). The AAC&U Creative Thinking Value Rubric (2009) defines creative thinking as "both the capacity to combine and synthesize existing ideas, images, or expertise in original ways and the experience of thinking, reacting, and working in an imaginative way, characterized by a high degree of innovation, divergent thinking, and risk taking" (AAC&U 2009). We designed this book to integrate creative thinking intentionally like a "rhizome," connecting and invigorating the process of composing (Lee and Carpenter 2016). This approach reinforces creative ways of thinking that are one of the crucial eight "habits of mind" supporting the development of students' writing and communication skills in higher education (Council of Writing Program Administrators 2011).

How do multimodal and creative thinking practices support career readiness?

Multimodal and creative thinking practices presented in this book help students bolster skills and ways of thinking that are aligned with career readiness competencies as defined by the National Association of Colleges and Employers (NACE). In practical terms, students learn and hone valuable skills and practices that are already identified as essential abilities sought by employers. NACE's competencies also point to the important application of the skills students learn in this book.

Multimodal and Creative Thinking Practices in *Design for Composition*
(based on NACE Career Readiness Competencies)

NACE Career Readiness Competencies	Multimodal and Creative Thinking Practices in *Design for Composition*
Communication "Clearly and effectively exchange information, ideas, facts, and perspectives with persons inside and outside of an organization."	Multimodal and creativity practices help students understand the importance of the various modes of communication (verbal, written, visual, nonverbal) by drawing attention to the different approaches, strategies, and applications across modalities. Multimodal and creativity practices help students employ and self-assess their communication skills. Multimodal and creativity practices help students consider the relevant audience and critically think about engagement and delivery.
Critical and Creative Thinking "Identify and respond to needs based upon an understanding of situational context and logical analysis of information."	Multimodal and creativity practices build critical and creative thinking by pushing students to explore decisions they make in communication, enhancing meta-cognition of the communication process, and encouraging rethinking and problem solving for more effective, creative application/delivery appropriate for a given context.

NACE Career Readiness Competencies	Multimodal and Creative Thinking Practices in *Design for Composition*
Equity and Inclusion "Demonstrate the awareness, attitude, knowledge, and skills required to equitably engage and include people from different local and global cultures."	Multimodal and creativity practices help students be mindful of language used to include and sometimes exclude audiences as well as help students consider different demographic groups, cultures, ideas, and ways of thinking when communicating.
Leadership "Recognize and capitalize on personal and team strengths to achieve organizational goals"	Multimodal and creativity practices ask students to collaborate with teammates to complete projects; share visions; and serve as role models when sharing tasks or projects with others.
Professionalism "Knowing work environments differ greatly, understand and demonstrate effective work habits, and the interest of the larger community and workspace."	Multimodal and creativity practices help students pay attention to detail, meet goals for projects, and demonstrate their work with others.
Teamwork "Build and maintain collaborative relationships to work effectively toward common goals, while appreciating diverse viewpoints and shared responsibilities."	Multimodal and creativity practices in this book emphasize teamwork and sharing; creativity practices in particular depend on feedback and collaboration for the completion of projects and reaching creativity goals.
Technology "Understand and leverage technologies ethically to enhance efficiencies, complete tasks, and accomplish goals."	Multimodal and creativity practices introduce students to a range of communication technologies as they explore how to be creative with modalities of expression; students learn to be comfortable with using technology to accomplish communication tasks and adapt to new or unfamiliar technologies.

ORGANIZATION

This workbook is organized to encourage creative thinking aligned with the Revised Bloom's Taxonomy in three areas, with a focus on 1) Observation, 2) Application, and 3) Creative Production. Observation focuses on the cognitive level of creativity, identifying and describing creativity as a process, skill, or craft. Through these chapters, students will learn to explain what they see, read, or touch in terms of creativity concepts. Chapters focusing on Application, however, allow students to apply creativity as process, skill, or craft. Through the exercises in the Application chapters, students explore understanding of creativity in one context and apply it in a new or unfamiliar context. Finally, in chapters focused on Creative Production students learn creativity as a heuristic craft, an approach to solve problems or achieve project objectives in innovative ways. Students begin with chapters focused on observation to application and production, practicing skills at each level. The workbook helps students move from experiencing creativity to intentional processes of designing creative multimodal projects and exploring ways to reflect on and apply these experiences to other situations in in-person, hybrid, or online courses.

In addition to enhancing their learning of creativity approaches, students will increasingly encounter projects that challenge these creativity and multimodal communication skills and move them toward complex design challenges. By completing the projects in this workbook, students will 1) become more aware of the composition process involved in a variety of modalities while working on projects; 2) become more aware of the creativity process involved in composition and communication; 3) understand the role of audience, purpose, and context in meaning making across a range of multimodal projects; and 4) analyze design principles, along with related art elements, as well as develop a more intentional communication approach for designing multimodal projects that include verbal, visual, tactile, oral/aural, and performance (body, nonverbal, and gestural) elements.

While each chapter provides unique creative projects, we offer sharing options and guidance for synchronous or asynchronous course delivery. Depending on how a class or group is asked to deliver a creative project, students may share the work virtually or in person. We also provide suggestions for sharing student work through freely available platforms or software, including Google Drive, Google Drawing, Padlet, PowerPoint, or other program platforms. For live activities (in person or synchronous), we have provided recommendations that students work in groups to analyze, produce, or reflect on their designs. For asynchronous interactions with classes or groups, we also make recommendations for adapting the projects. We suggest tools in each chapter that allow students to complete the projects in any course delivery format.

HOW TO USE THIS BOOK

The workbook format of *Design for Composition* allows instructors to choose from among a range of engaging activities for use across teaching, learning, and instructional contexts and deliveries. Instructors can incorporate it in several ways to support student learning:

- To complement course content in areas related to writing, communication, or multimodal composing;
- To supplement exercises that bring active and experiential learning opportunities to students;
- As a workbook complement to existing course texts; and
- As a guide with exercises to expand on course content.

Instructors will also find that the workbook can function flexibly across purposes in or among these areas. The creative projects found in each chapter can encourage students to explore processes that allow them to learn and experiment with practices that can be applied to composing, communication, and multimodal projects at the course, module, or exercise levels.

At the course level, the workbook can be adopted to provide students with interactive experiences, as each chapter can work as a stand-alone resource or as a guide for creative production. However, instructors can also incorporate chapter exercises into the course to structure creative opportunities for students. Chapters are designed as modular and, therefore, can be configured or reconfigured to fit the goals or learning outcomes of the course or composing experience.

Course Modality and Delivery

This workbook is designed to be responsive to in-person, online (synchronous and asynchronous), and hybrid (in-person and online), and flexible modalities. Recognizing the need to give instructors ultimate flexibility in how the workbook is used and adapted to best suit student learning, we ensure that each chapter contains a rich background, compelling examples, and engaging creative exercises. The exercises, importantly, encourage collaboration and peer-to-peer learning. They also challenge students to think creatively in ways that extend learning from the classroom. Instructors will find that the workbook integrates with online or on-ground pedagogical approaches as well. Each chapter features unique projects that fit multiple delivery approaches.

Using the Workbook

Instructors will find multiple options for using this workbook to expand their curriculum.

Instructors can begin by scheduling the workbook or a chapter within it as a component of the course. They can also provide students with access and planning time in advance as the course allows. The creative projects include an estimated timeframe within which the exercise can be completed. Instructors have the option to apply that time limit to the project or modify it for their course purposes.

The chapters and creative projects are designed to also give instructors the flexibility to design their courses around them. That is, the workbook provides a structure for lessons in the course, along with scaffolding to support instruction. This option allows instructors to create an interactive, workshop-oriented approach to teaching, allowing students to experience these creative projects, to plan, and to reflect on their experiences as part of the development of the course itself.

We encourage instructors to help prepare students for creative thinking. Creativity thrives in safe, supportive, and encouraging learning environments where students feel that they can explore new ideas, thoughts, and processes while embracing some of the unknown in the process. Some students will come to the exercises in the workbook without having thought deeply about their creative abilities, while others will feel that they are coming to the class (and the experiences in the workbook) with more experience and confidence in their creative potential and prior experience.

The workbook makes the process transparent by helping students, as Mary-Ann Winkelmes, Allison Boye, and Szanne Tapp suggest (2019), understand the how and the why of creative thinking. This aspect of creativity is critical to student engagement. It encourages buy-in and helps students become metacognitive thinkers by understanding the ways that they learn through

1. planning a creative project;
2. designing a creative project; and
3. reflecting on the process on their own and with others.

We encourage ample time for intentional reflection and debrief as well as showcasing creative projects during or after class time or, if teaching in fully online or hybrid modalities, through digital displays or archives. Instructors can create meaningful (and enjoyable) learning experiences when scaffolding course experiences around these creative projects.

CHAPTERS

Each chapter is designed to weave modality (visual, oral, textual, etc.) with the development of four cognitive levels of creativity (observation, application, evaluation, and production), and rhetorical learning outcomes designed for the activity.

Chapter One is entitled "Visualizing and Feeling Observation: Found Creativity Through Elements of Art." The aim of this chapter is to introduce students to the visual modality through five art elements (line, color, shape, texture, and space). Students are asked to interact with objects found in everyday contexts and observe creativity in how art elements are used in visual communication. Main learning outcome: Through this visual creativity project, students learn to recognize and identify art elements and aspects of creativity needed for communicating meaning or eliciting responses and interactions.

Chapter Two, "Visualizing Observation: Understanding Design Principles through Vintage Ads and Posters," builds on what students learned about art elements in Chapter One, by introducing them to design principles. The visual creativity project asks students to identify how four classic design principles (unity, balance, focalization, and repetition) may be employed in print ads in free online databases. Main learning outcome: Through the observation of creativity, students learn to think about the rhetorical role of design and design principles to persuade in print advertising.

In Chapter 3, "Feeling Observation: Touch Test in Product Design," students are introduced to haptics (interaction with things that you touch or hold in your hands) and the role of texture and touch in aesthetics, value, and experience of a product. How do touch design features shape our interpretation and response to products? Is it different depending on culture and country? How can touch be "designed" for a target audience? Main learning outcome: The observation of tactile creativity increases student awareness of tactile communication by helping them identify the strategic use of texture and touch in common objects.

Chapter 4, "Speaking Application: Vocal Expression," invites students to identify and apply vocalics or nonverbal vocal expression that contributes to oral communication. Focusing on vocalics, students are asked to pay attention to pitch, rate, volume, articulation, pronunciation, and even pauses by analyzing the vocalics of well-known speakers who read Edgar Allen Poe's *The Raven*. Students, then, are asked to read it themselves and analyze the vocalics in their own voice. Main learning outcome: Students not only observe how vocalics can change the way listeners receive and interpret a message but learn to apply their understanding to their own vocal expression or technique.

In Chapter 5, "Interacting Application: Thinking/Rethinking App Icons for an Everyday Activity," students move beyond observation to application. In this visual project, students are asked to design an icon for an invented app involving an everyday activity. The goal of this project is to help students think creatively about what makes memorable symbols as well as create symbols that succinctly tell a story of an activity. Main learning outcome: Students learn the creative process of creating symbols by prototyping multiple versions of the concept and exploring creativity in visual storytelling.

In Chapter 6, "Touching Evaluation: Creativity in Clothing and Texture," students generate a texture-based creativity rubric and evaluate the creativity of found texture (specifically clothing). Through the process, they try to answer these questions: What makes certain textures more creative than others? How does texture impact the social messages carried in the design of clothing? Students critically reflect on specific types of visual and tactile texture, produce a rubric for evaluating creative texture, and evaluate items of clothes that use texture creatively. Main learning outcome: Students increase critical awareness and understanding of the basic components of visual and tactile texture and appreciate texture as an element of design with rhetorical implications.

In Chapter 7, "Speaking and Writing Application: Ventriloquy and Rhetorical Devices," students learn to apply creativity in an oral project. Students are introduced to rhetorical devices by identifying and modeling the structure of classic speeches. They practice applying rhetorical devices themselves by selecting a famous speech, identifying one or two specific rhetorical devices, and imitating the rhetorical style using their own words and contexts. Main learning outcome: Students will gain a better understanding of the power of rhetorical devices in speech and how to apply them.

Chapter 8, "Performing Application: Instrumental Theme Songs for the News," focuses students' attention on an application of an aural project. Students explore creative production music for newscasts to identify how abstract sounds brand a news organization's personality and set a tone/theme. Students are asked to listen to sound clips of newscast theme songs, then create their own news soundtrack based on the type of news they imagine it is conveying and the audience. Main learning outcome: Through this aural creative project, students identify and apply aural modality.

In Chapter 9, "Composing Production: Making Your Own Portmanteau," students produce a creative oral/written project. Portmanteau, described by Lewis Carroll's Humpty Dumpty as "two meanings packed up into one word," is a means by which a playful combination of sound features hint at parts of words we recognize and know. Creativity skills needed to make these new words are valuable and exist beyond literature. This chapter asks students to explore sound and meaning by creating new words that combine the sounds of familiar words. Main learning outcome: Students hone creativity skills and increase their understanding of speech sounds and perceived meaning. They will study a model portmanteau, apply divergent thinking by generating portmanteau words, use convergent thinking to narrow down choices, and reflect critically on the whole process.

Chapter 10, "Seeing Production: Album Art and Discovering Typography," presents a visual/aural creativity project. The chapter introduces students to the idea of typography and the way type and graphic design impact how we read and feel about a word. In this multisensory creativity project, students convert one modality (sound) to another (visual): They will be creating an album cover of their favorite sound using only typeface, layout, and color. Main learning outcome: Students increase their understanding of the rhetorical affordances of typeface by using type and graphics to communicate meaning of a song.

Finally, in Chapter 11, "Performing Production: Contact [Object] Improvisation," students increase body language awareness and explore creative body movements by performing contact improvisation. The project introduces students to contact improvisation, experimental movements in dance that help the performer become more sensitive to touch and their own body patterns. Main learning outcome: Through contact improvisation, students explore body movement possibilities and increase physicality and awareness of space. Students reflect on how their experience and awareness impact their live presentation skills in light of gestures, body language, motion, and the affordances of presentation spaces.

REFERENCES

Anderson, Daniel. 2008. "The Low Bridge to High Benefits: Entry-Level Multimedia, Literacies, and Motivation." *Computers and Composition* 25 (1): 40–60. doi:10.1016/j.compcom.2007.09.006

Association of American Colleges and Universities (AAC&U). 2009. *Creative Thinking VALUE Rubric*. Washington, DC: Association of American Colleges and Universities.

Carey, Linda J., and Linda Flower. 1989. *Foundations for Creativity in the Writing Process: Rhetorical Representations of Ill-Defined Problems*. Berkeley, CA: Center for the Study of Writing.

Council of Writing Program Administrators. 2011. *Framework for Success in Postsecondary Writing*. https://bit.ly/cwpaframework.

Doorley, Scott, and Scott Witthoft. 2012. *Make Space: How to Set the Stage for Creative Collaboration*. Hoboken, NJ: Wiley.

Edwards-Groves, Christine. 2012. "Interactive Creative Technologies: Changing Learning Practices and Pedagogies in Writing Classrooms." *Australian Journal of Language and Literacy* 35 (1): 99–113.

Elbow, Peter. 1983. "Teaching Thinking by Teaching Writing." *Change* 15 (6): 37–40.

Flower, Linda, and John R. Hayes. 1977. "Problem-solving Strategies and the Writing Process." *College English* 39 (4): 449–61.

—. 1980. "The Cognition of Discovery: Defining a Rhetorical Problem. *College Composition and Communication* 31 (4): 21-32.

—. 1981. "A Cognitive Process Theory of Writing." *College Composition and Communication* 32 (4): 365–87.

Kress, Gunther. 2000. "Multimodality: Challenges to Thinking About Languages." *TESOL Quarterly* 34 (2): 337–40.

Kress, Gunther, and Theo van Leeuwen. 2001. *Multimodal Discourse: The Modes and Media of Contemporary Communication.* London: Arnold.

Lee, Sohui, and Russell Carpenter. 2015. "Creative Thinking for Twenty-First Century Composing Practices: Creativity Pedagogies Across Disciplines." Special issue "Create, Perform, Write: WAC, WID, and the Performing and Visual Arts!" *Across the Disciplines: A Journal of Language, Learning, and Academic Writing* 12 (4). doi: 10.37514/ATD-J.2015.12.4.12

—. 2016. "Future Pedagogies of Applied Creative Thinking in Multiliteracy Centers: How Creative Thinking 'Opens the Ways' for Better Habits of Mind." In *The Future Scholar: Researching & Teaching the Frameworks for Writing and Information Literacy*, edited by. Randall McCLure and James P. Purdy, 223–48. Medford, NJ: Information Today.

National Association of Colleges and Employers (NACE). 2014. https://www.naceweb.org/.

Newcomb, Matthew. 2012. "Sustainability as a Design Principle for Composition: Situational Creativity as a Habit of Mind." *College Composition and Communication* 63 (4): 593–615.

New London Group. 1996. "A Pedagogy of Multiliteracies: Designing Social Futures." *Harvard Educational Review* 66 (Spring): 60–92.

Purdy, James. 2014. "What Can Design Thinking Offer Writing Studies?" *College Composition and Communication* 64 (4): 612–41.

Selfe, Richard J., and Cynthia L. Selfe. 2008. "'Convince me!' Valuing Multimodal Literacies and Composing Public Service Announcements." *Theory into Practice* 47 (2): 83–92.

Serafini, Frank. 2011. "Expanding Perspectives for Comprehending Visual Images in Multimodal Texts." *Journal of Adolescent & Adult Literacy* 54 (5): 342–50.

Takayoshi, Pamela, and Cynthia L. Selfe, Cynthia. 2007. "Chapter 1: 'Thinking about Multimodality.'" *Multimodal Composition: Resources for Teachers*, edited by Gail E. Hawisher and Cynthia Selfe, 1–12. Hampton Press.

Winkelmes, Mary-Ann, Allison Boye, and Suzanne Tapp. 2019. *Transparent Design in Higher Education Teaching and Leadership: A Guide to Implementing the Transparency Framework Institution-Wide to Improve Learning and Retention.* Sterling, VA: Stylus.

Wolfe, Silvia, and Rosie Flewitt. 2010. "New Technologies, New Multimodal Literacy Practices and Young Children's Metacognitive Development." *Cambridge Journal of Education* 40 (4): 387–99.

1 VISUALIZING AND FEELING OBSERVATION
FOUND CREATIVITY THROUGH ELEMENTS OF ART

"Creativity is as important as literacy" — Sir Ken Robinson

SET THE SCENE

What elements make an object creative? **Art elements** such as line, color, shape, texture, and space often intentionally contribute to an object's design and **creativity**. This project—"Found Creativity"—suggests that you can better understand creative designs of objects by archiving and reflecting on the role of art elements in communication. Through observation of and interaction with objects, you learn the affordances—possibilities and meanings—of art elements in design and the **design process**. While art elements are often recognized in paintings and sculptures, for example, this project encourages you to recognize these elements in everyday objects and items (e.g., pens, cups, books, and furniture). Through this process, you will gain a better understanding of art elements and their role in creative designs.

CONNECT TO CREATIVITY

Chapter 1 introduces creativity by asking you to identify how elements of art, which you see in your daily life (i.e. in your community, home, or workspace) contribute to the creative design of objects. You will focus on specific strategies of art elements employed through either or both visual and tactile (touch) modalities. Over the course of five days, you will take pictures of objects or artifacts that distinctively use the following art elements: line, color, shape, texture, and space. At the end of the week, you will propose a definition of creativity based on your observations and interactions with these objects.

By completing this activity, you will:

- **Discover** how elements of art (line, color, shape, texture, and space) may be used in a creative way for a range of day-to-day purposes.
- **Analyze and compare** creative art elements in visual or tactile modalities.
- **Reflect** on each of the creative objects you've chosen by explaining why it is "creative."
- **Propose** a definition of creativity based on your observations and interactions with art elements.

LEVEL UP

Free Tools

To help you archive found creative objects, we've assembled two free sites. Use these sites as a starting point for this project.

Tool	URL	Description
Google Drawings	In Google Drive, click on "New" and choose Google Drawings under "More."	Google Drawings is a collaborative visual "pad" on which you can drag and drop images and add text. In addition, you can create lines, arrows, scribbles, shapes, and other visual cues for diagrams. Here's a link to creative uses of Google Drawings: http://www.makeuseof.com/tag/8-creative-uses-google-drawings-shouldnt-ignore/
Padlet.com	www.padlet.com	Padlet is a free, online, collaborative web-based pad. You can add pictures, notes, videos, and sound clips to be seen holistically on one padlet. You can also share or ask others to add to your padlet.

Learn More

In the section below, learn more about how designers are creative with color, pattern, shapes, texture, and/or space. A number of sources feature examples based on productions or research.

General Definition of Elements of Art (Line, Color, Shape, Texture, and Space):

The **J. Paul Getty Museum** provides a longer definition of elements of art that are useful to know when identifying how these elements are applied in objects of design: https://www.getty. edu/education/teachers/building_lessons/formal_analysis.html.

The J. Paul Getty Museum also provides a useful one-page summary of the element of art: https://www.getty.edu/education/teachers/building_lessons/elements_art.pdf.

Usability.gov also provides a definition of basic elements of visual design (art elements). It also provides a brief summary of design principles as it might be applied to web design usability— but this is also useful for visual designs from static print format: https://www.usability.gov/ what-and-why/visual-design.html.

Line

KQED provides examples of how artists use a variety of "line" techniques to communicate their message. Watch this video to see how they might be applied in everyday objects and items that we use: https://www.youtube.com/watch?v=BDePyEFT1gQ.

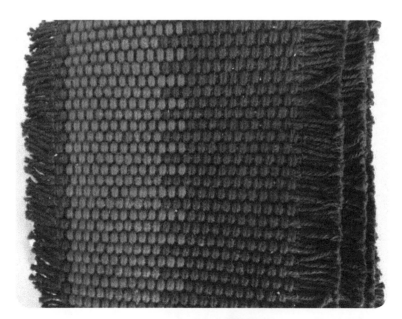

Figure 1: Line example of an everyday object: Office Coaster.

CHAPTER ONE: FOUND CREATIVITY

Color

Understandinggraphics.com lists ten ways color is used in visual design. Understanding the uses of color can help you employ it more creatively: http://understandinggraphics.com/design/10-reasons-to-use-color/.

Figure 2: Color example of an everyday object for enhancing mood: Nightlight.

Shape (2D) / Form (3D)

Getty Museum provides a handout/worksheet that introduces the concept of "shape": http://www.getty.edu/education/teachers/building_lessons/introducing_shape.pdf.

Creativebloq.com offers examples for the creative use of negative space as "shape" in two dimensions: http://www.creativebloq.com/art/art-negative-space-8133765.

Figure 3: A creative shape example of an everyday object: the book is designed to look like a 3-D block.

CHAPTER ONE: FOUND CREATIVITY

Texture (Tactile and Visual)

Tactile Texture: Through a YouTube video, Vaughn Stephenson introduces the effective use of tactile texture in the visual arts. This video provides you with the sense of the different ways tactile texture is used. It also provides a comparison against visual texture (how the artist visually depicts how something might feel): https://www.youtube.com/watch?v=aUuN4M64bhA.

Figure 4: Texture example of an everyday object: container.

Space (2D and 3D)

Two-dimensional representation and three-dimensional use of space can be understood in the composition of drawings, art, and sculptures. Positive and negative space is used are visual arts to convey meaning, tone, and perspective. See KQED Arts video "Element of Art: Space" which explores the role of space in two dimensional and three dimensional visual arts: https://www.youtube.com/watch?v=U11B_0FCn6o.

Figure 5: Example of the use of space in a library lounge area.

CREATIVE PROJECT

Found Creativity Through Elements of Art

BEFORE YOU BEGIN

Know the five elements of art that you will be archiving and describing in this activity: Line, Color, Texture, and Shape. We recommend that you read the J. Paul Getty Museum's definition of the five elements of art under the "Learn More" section of this chapter. You can use the one-page handout from the Getty Museum as a guide when you are searching for objects.

Total Estimated Time: 1.5 hours for Doing and Reflecting.

Skills: Understanding of design elements, recognition of creativity through artistic elements in visual and tactile forms.

Sharing Options: Depending on how your class or group is asked to deliver this project, you may be sharing the work virtually or in person. We suggest sharing your collection of found creativity through Google Drawing, Padlet, PowerPoint, or another program platform.

Synchronous/Asynchronous: This activity can be conducted both synchronously and asynchronously.

I. CREATIVITY: DOING

"Where do new ideas come from? The answer is simple: differences. Creativity comes from unlikely juxtapositions." — Nicholas Negroponte

Overview

In this exercise, you will collect photos of found objects that apply to one of the five elements of art. You will assemble the photos in a program like Google Drawing. In addition, you will analyze each of the found objects using the instructions we provide below. The goal of this project is to explore objects that seem to exhibit creativity through the elements of art. Have fun finding these objects!

Directions

1. **Print** the J. Paul Getty Museum's one-page handout to help you identify the elements of art in objects. Focus on Line, Shape, Space, Color, and Texture.

2. **Find and photograph** found objects that apply each of the five elements of art (Line, Shape, Space, Color, and Texture) in a creative way using a smartphone or other digital devices. You'll look for a creative use of an element of art in objects, things, buildings, etc. that you see every day in public and work spaces, or in your home. The objects should not be intentionally an art piece; that is, the primary purpose of the object is something other than being a work of art. For instance, a pen's primary purpose as an object is to be used as a writing instrument, but it may be designed with art elements in mind.

3. **Upload photos** of creative objects onto Google Drawing or a similar platform.

4. **Create a caption for each photo** briefly describing the object in its context and analyzing the object in terms of its creative use of art elements. Write it out in Google Drawing and use the table below as a guideline.

The tables below identify each element of art in your creative found objects. See Examples 1 and 2 for reference.

Day One	Find an object that creatively uses the art element: Line
Name of Object	
Description of Object in its Context	
Analysis (2 to 3 lines)	

Day Two	Find an object that creatively uses the art element: Shape
Name of Object	
Description of Object in its Context	
Analysis (2 to 3 lines)	

Day Three	Find an object that creatively uses the art element: Space
Name of Object	
Description of Object in its Context	
Analysis (2 to 3 lines)	

Day Four	Find an object that creatively uses the art element: Color
Name of Object	
Description of Object in its Context	
Analysis (2 to 3 lines)	

Day Five	Find an object that creatively uses the art element: Texture
Name of Object	
Description of Object in its Context	
Analysis (2 to 3 lines)	

Project Examples

Created through Google Drawings, these figures are samples of chapter 1's creative project that presents images of everyday items that exemplify elements of art found through five days. Each image includes a short analysis of the found object.

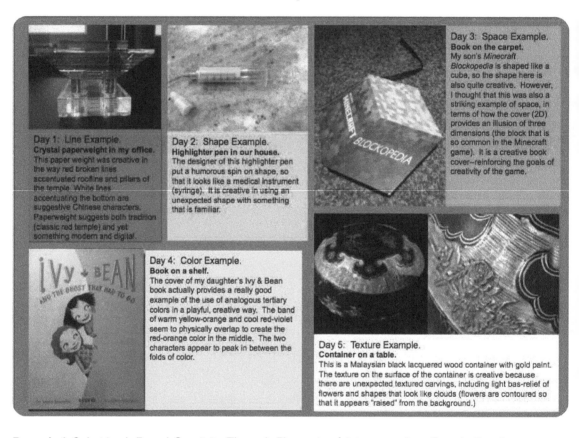

Day 1: Line Example.
Crystal paperweight in my office.
This paper weight was creative in the way red broken lines accentuated roofline and pillars of the temple. White lines accentuating the bottom are suggestive Chinese characters. Paperweight suggests both tradition (classic red temple) and yet something modern and digital.

Day 2: Shape Example.
Highlighter pen in our house.
The designer of this highlighter pen put a humorous spin on shape, so that it looks like a medical instrument (syringe). It is creative in using an unexpected shape with something that is familiar.

Day 3: Space Example.
Book on the carpet.
My son's *Minecraft Blockopedia* is shaped like a cube, so the shape here is also quite creative. However, I thought that this was also a striking example of space, in terms of how the cover (2D) provides an illusion of three dimensions (the block that is so common in the Minecraft game). It is a creative book cover--reinforcing the goals of creativity of the game.

Day 4: Color Example.
Book on a shelf.
The cover of my daughter's Ivy & Bean book actually provides a really good example of the use of analogous tertiary colors in a playful, creative way. The band of warm yellow-orange and cool red-violet seem to physically overlap to create the red-orange color in the middle. The two characters appear to peak in between the folds of color.

Day 5: Texture Example.
Container on a table.
This is a Malaysian black lacquered wood container with gold paint. The texture on the surface of the container is creative because there are unexpected textured carvings, including light bas-relief of flowers and shapes that look like clouds (flowers are contoured so that it appears "raised" from the background.)

Example 1: Sohui Lee's Found Creativity Through Elements of Art, created on Google Drawing.

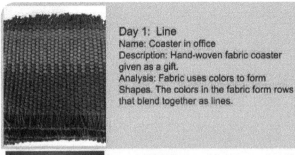

Day 1: Line
Name: Coaster in office
Description: Hand-woven fabric coaster given as a gift.
Analysis: Fabric uses colors to form
Shapes. The colors in the fabric form rows that blend together as lines.

Day 4: Texture
Name: Fluffy ottoman
Description: Fabric pieces give the object a fun, whimsical look
Analysis: The object incorporates small fabric pieces to give it
Shapes: Rectangular fabric helps to give the object a rounded and comfortable look

Day 2: Color
Name: Night light in hallway
Description: Circular shape and blue color make the object reflect light from the bulb
Analysis: Light and color give dimension to the round shape
Shapes: Rounded edges and fragmented lines give complexity to the object

Day 3: Shape
Name: Ballerina slipper bank
Description: Bank shaped as ballerina slippers with 3D and color
Analysis: Shape of slippers conveys playful tone and offers an unexpected object for containing coins.

Day 5: Space
Name: Lounge area in Broome Library, Children's section
Description: The lounge space outlined by a red floor mat with benches and cushions.
Analysis: The space occupied by these objects is creative because the shape and proportions of the cushions and benches are unexpected. The spines of "books" (or benches) give the illusion of being books being stuck into the floor.

Example 2: Russell Carpenter's Found Creativity Through Elements of Art, created on Google Drawing.

II. CREATIVITY: REFLECTING

Reflection is an important metacognitive process of learning because it helps you recall and identify ideas and concepts you learned and articulate how you understand them. You may be asked to provide an oral or written reflection in response to the following questions, either virtually or in person. If you are in a team, work with your team members to answer the questions below:

1. How are the objects that you or your team have selected creatively using art elements? Share the ways you think the objects differently exemplify creativity.

2. Next, report on how you will look at the design and creativity of objects differently in the future. Based on your current observations, how would you define "creativity"?

2 VISUAL OBSERVATION
UNDERSTANDING DESIGN PRINCIPLES THROUGH VINTAGE ADS AND POSTERS

"The elements and principles of design are not a recipe for creating a perfect piece of visual communication, but a knowledge and understanding of these tools opens the doors to a myriad of options and opportunities that may have otherwise remained hidden. Fine artists, graphic artists, web and game designers, architects, landscape designers, town planners, florists, fashion designers, sign writers, industrial designers—the list goes on and on. . . . An understanding of the elements and principles of design is a vital step to making sense of what we see and create." — John Lovett, Artist

SET THE SCENE

In Chapter 1, you learned about the role of art elements (line, color, shape, and texture) in creativity and communication. One way to think about art elements is that they are "bricks" used to create a larger, intentional structure of meaning (the "building"). Design principles are critical guides for organizing art elements in effective and meaningful visual design. Through this activity, you will gain a better understanding of basic design principles and their role in conveying persuasive, emotionally powerful messages.

Figure 1: "Orient Cafe Restaurant" poster (1926) by W. Knittel illustrates the use of art elements (color) and design principle (unity).

CONNECT TO CREATIVITY

Chapter 2 builds on Chapter 1 and introduces you to design principles through the use of vintage print ads or posters. There are many design principles, but in this exercise you will focus on exploring four in particular: **unity**, **balance**, **focalization**, and **repetition**. In this challenge, you will be asked to collect five ads representing one design principle, of which you will choose three to present as examples in which design principles help convey the message and are applied rhetorically. You will then contribute to a Google Slideshow to track creative observations, which you will share with a class or small group to explain creative uses of design principles in these vintage print ads and posters. Understanding uses of design principles through vintage print ads and posters allows you to experience a range of possible approaches and strategies for appealing to viewers. You will begin to express ways in which these strategies are creative.

During this activity, you will

- **Discover** how design principles (unity, balance, focalization, and repetition) may be used in a creative way in print advertisements for a range of meaning/messages.
- **Analyze and compare** one design principle employed in at least five print ads (ultimately analyzing two print ads in detail).
- **Reflect** on three of the print ads you've chosen by explaining how a visual design principle is employed to creatively convey the message.
- **Propose** on what you learned from others (classmates or teammates). How do their analyses of design principles differ from yours?

LEVEL UP

Free Tools

To help you share and analyze vintage advertisements and posters, we've assembled four free sites. Use these sites as a starting point for this project.

Tool	URL	Description
Google Presentation	In Google Drive, click on "New" and choose "Google Slides." Students may copy our template for describing and analyzing the ads or posters: http://tinyurl.com/ch2-slideshowtemplate	Google Slides is a collaborative slide-design platform. It allows you to create shareable slideshows and comment on features of the slideshow.
Library of Congress, World War I Posters	https://www.loc.gov/pictures/collection/wwipos/	Vintage World War I Posters (1000+) held in the Library of Congress. On the home page, click on "View All" to see the collection.
Ad*Access	https://repository.duke.edu/dc/adaccess	From Duke University Library Collections, Ad*Access provides over 7,000 U.S. and Canadian advertisements covering five product categories - Beauty and Hygiene, Radio, Television, Transportation, and World War II propaganda (1911–1955).

Learn More

In the section below, learn more about how designers are creative with principles of unity, balance, focalization, and repetition. A number of sources feature examples based on productions or research.

General Definition of Design Principles of Unity, Balance, Focalization, and Repetition

The **J. Paul Getty Museum** provides a handout on general principles of design in a work of art. The Getty discusses focalization in terms of emphasis. It also breaks down repetition more specifically in terms of repetition, pattern, and rhythm: https://bit.ly/designforcomposition37.

Unity

The design principle of unity involves using a range of art elements to create harmony in the design: this includes the use of color, shapes, texture, and contrast. Read more and see examples: https://venngage.com/blog/design-principle-unity/.

Figure 2:
"Carnaval 1936" (1936) poster illustrates the design principle of unity through color, shapes, and texture.

Balance (also discussed as symmetry)

Design principle of balance is used in landscape, photograph, and other visual arts through the arrangement of what designers call "visual weight" or positive and negative space. *Smashing Magazine* (an online magazine for web designers and developers) provides an article that explores different types of balance and provides excellent examples: https://bit.ly/designforcomposition-principles.

Figure 3: "Bali Das Wunderland" poster (1927) is an example of asymmetrical balance where there is unequal visual weight on one side of the composition (deep blue color) compared to the other (lighter color with text).

Focalization (also discussed as focal points, emphasis, and dominance)

Steven Bradley discusses and provides examples of focalization through dominance, focal points, and hierarchy: https://bit.ly/designforcomposition-dominance

Figure 4: "Christmas U.S. Naval Hospital" (1944) illustrates the use of dominance in the title "Christmas." Art elements that can be used for dominance include size, shape, color, value, depth, texture, and orientation. Here it is size, color, font (shape), and contrast.

Repetition (also discussed as rhythm)

Artist John Lovett explains the design principle of **repetition** and provides visual examples in its application and use of variety of art elements (line, shape, color, and texture) in photograph, architecture, and other visual arts: https://www.johnlovett.com/repetition.

Figure 5: "Phalanx 1. Ausstellung" poster (1901) announces an art exhibition. The illustration on the poster include design principles of repetition through repeated figures (soldiers), spears, columns, and even the colors blue and aqua that are woven through the image and the letters in "Phalanx" and "Ausstellung."

CHAPTER TWO: ADS AND POSTERS

CREATIVE PROJECT

Understanding Design Principles through Vintage Ads and Posters

BEFORE YOU BEGIN

Know the four principles of design and a variety of art elements are used to achieve the design: unity, balance, focalization (or emphasis/dominance), and repetition. We recommend that you read the J. Paul Getty Museum's definition of the general principles of design and the description and examples of design principles working with art elements under the "Learn More" section of this chapter. In addition, we recommend that you refer to examples of principles using art elements as a guide when you are analyzing the application of design principles for this activity.

Class Activity Description

This project requires approximately two hours, one to research the designs using the databases we have provided and the other to share and reflect to a class or group after you have archived and written about your vintage designs. You will need time to upload and analyze the visuals you have selected, which you will develop using Google Slides that you will share.

Total Estimated Time:

- 1 hour for Creativity: Doing;
- 1 hour Creativity: Sharing and Reflecting [recommend activity after the vintage designs are collected and ready to share].

Skills: Understanding of elements of design, recognition of creativity in design principles used in vintage art and posters.

Sharing Options: Depending on how your class or group is asked to deliver this project, you may be sharing the work virtually or in person. We suggest sharing your collection of found vintage designs using Google Slides or another platform that your instructor identifies.

I. CREATIVITY: DOING

"Design is the intermediary between information and understanding."
— Hans Hoffman, Artist

Overview

Identify and analyze design principles that apply elements of art. Your instructor will be asking you to apply what you know about design principles by explaining how they are being used in vintage ads and posters. You may be assigned a specific design principle or you may be given a choice to select a design principle. Ultimately, your goal is to share five ads/posters and analyze three that illustrate the use of the design principle applying different art elements. Please see below for examples of completed Google slides with design principle analysis of vintage ads and posters.

Databases for Vintage Ads and Posters

- Library of Congress, "Posters: World War I Posters:" https://www.loc.gov/pictures/collection/wwipos/.
- Duke University's Ad*Access: https://repository.duke.edu/dc/adaccess.

Directions

1. **Access** the J. Paul Getty Museum's one-page handout on principles of design to help you identify the way balance, focalization, repetition, or unity is being used. Don't forget that focalization is described in a variety of ways (J. Paul Getty Museum calls focalization "Emphasis"; Steven Bradley describes focalization as "Dominance")
2. **Select FIVE ads or posters** in the databases that we've provided (or in the database that your instructor provides).
3. **Save and upload** the screenshot of the ads or posters onto Google Slides. We recommend that you use the vintage ad table to fill in your analysis and then create a Google Slide using the Project Examples as a reference.
4. **Fill out a table or questions in the template** describing the ad/poster.

Use the following tables to guide you in identifying each element of art in your vintage poster or ad. See Examples 1 and 2 for reference.

Vintage Ad	[Provide name of title.]
Source	[Provide artist, description, year, location/database.]
Visual Design Principle	[Identify the design principles provided in this chapter and the art element.]
Ad/Poster Summary	[Summary of the ad.]
Principle Analysis	[Explain the design principle and how it is used with one or two art elements. Explain how the principle makes the ad more persuasive.]

Vintage Ad	
Source	
Visual Design Principle	
Ad/Poster Summary	
Principle Analysis	

Project Examples

Created through Google Slides, the Chapter 2 creative project examples present analyses of design principles applied through vintage print advertisements.

VINTAGE AD #4

Source: Emerson Phonograph, print ad, 1920, Vintage Ad Browser database

Visual Design Principle: Focalization by size and repetition

Ad Summary: The ad for Emerson Phonograph sells the product as a state of art technology in sound quality because it was built based on "science," and that this product will enhance listener's enjoyment of music.

Principle Analysis: The focus of the print ad is the illustration of the Emerson Phonograph, located on the lower right corner of the page. It is focalized by the dominant **size** of the product (exceeding the size by anything else on the page). In addition, it is focalized by **repeated** concentric circles with the center point being the circular horn of the phonograph. Concentric circles represents sound radiating from the phonograph (science-based technology) but also helps the eye focus on the device and its design.

Focalization, in this ad, calls attention to the product but also reinforces its cutting edge technology in sound.

Emerson Phonograph Ad Queen Anne Model (1920)

Example 1: Sohui Lee's Slide #4 created on Google Slides: https://bit.ly/designforcomposition-vintage-ad.

VINTAGE POSTER #4

Identifying source: The Hegeman Print N.Y., 1917, poster, Library of Congress
Visual design principle: Unity - direction
Poster summary: The poster promotes the screening of war-time films using the light of the ship to highlight the title much as a spotlight might highlight the title of a movie in Hollywood.
Principle analysis: The design employs unity to create emphasis in the direction of the title. The use of light signifies the importance of the title used on the poster.

Example 2: Russell Carpenter's Slide #4 on Google Slides: https://bit.ly/designforcompositionvintage.

II. CREATIVITY: SHARING AND REFLECTING

Reflection is an important metacognitive process of learning because it helps you recall and identify ideas and concepts you learned and articulate how you understand them. You may be asked to provide an oral or written reflection in response to the following questions, either virtually or in person.

The following are ways to share and reflect with others. If you are in a team, work with your team members to answer the questions below. Here are a few ideas for how you might share the design principles project.

- You might form small groups and share your Google Slides and analysis. Each group can then elect one person to share the best examples to the entire class.
- The instructor might ask you to draw names of students by lottery to present their Google slides and analysis.

- You might present their Google Slide of design principles to the entire class.
- The instructor might review your work after class and select specific projects by students to be discussed the next time class meets.
- You might post your analysis on a blog and respond to a classmate/teammate's analysis online.

III. CREATIVITY: REFLECTING

If working on this project individually, you might answer the following questions:

Oral Reflection: Peer Feedback

Provide feedback after reviewing the Google Slides created by others. The following are questions you can ask your peer(s) or teammates:

Design Principles and Art Elements

- How does the effect of different art elements impact the way a design principle was represented?
- How are the analyses of the design principles with art elements different or similar to yours?
- Have they noticed anything different from your analysis?

Creative Sample

- Reflecting back on the print ad/poster design you've selected, how are they creative?

Report Back

- At the end of the reflection period, report on how the understanding of design principles impact the way you look at the design of print ads/posters. As a result of your observations, how would you use design principles to define "creativity?"

FEELING OBSERVATION
TOUCH TEST IN PRODUCT DESIGN

"Design is not just what it looks like and feels like. Design is how it works." — Steve Jobs

SET THE SCENE

How does design feel in the hand? How does an object's feel or texture contribute to the ways you interact with it or, as Steve Jobs puts it, "how it works"?

Figure 1: Fabrica De Borracha Luso-Belga

In Chapter 1, you learned basic design principles and their role in conveying messages through line, color, shape, texture, and space. Although there are many ways to think about the design of products, we often overlook their creativity and features, particularly the subtle feature of touch, because we interact with these items daily. Through this chapter, you will gain a better understanding of **haptics** (interaction with things you touch or hold in your hand). Designing for texture and touch might involve asking the following questions:

- How does the product feel to hold and use?
- How does the product's "feel" impact the way we think about the experience (of using it)?
- How does the product's "feel" impact the way we think about the product's value or quality?
- How does the product's "feel" shape the way we think about its aesthetic appeal?

Answers to these questions can help you understand creative tactile product design.

CONNECT TO CREATIVITY

Figure 2: Men's Cologne

Chapter 3 asks you to explore more deeply how to use touch to interpret and respond to product design, in particular, perfume and cologne bottles or packages.

The selling of perfume and cologne relies heavily on how a consumer "feels" about the perfume and cologne—and, it depends on advertising working in conjunction with the product design of the bottle and package to reinforce the ideas or experiences that become associated with a perfume or cologne. The touch sensory activity in this chapter will help you increase your awareness of how tactile experiences contribute to the marketing of a product. How does the mass, shape, contours, and textures of the object shape how we feel about it, who would feel attracted to it, or what "attitudes" it represents? The blind touch test exercise may also remind us how subtly the tactile nature of things influences what we think of the object—and whether the tactile message reinforces the visual argument.

By completing this activity, you will

- **Discover** how designers use texture, shape, and mass in creative ways to convey a range of meaning/messages.
- **Analyze** one perfume or cologne bottle in terms of texture, shape, or mass to determine 1) the target audience, and 2) the message being related about the product.
- **Reflect** on whether or not the perfume or cologne that you've chosen matches your analysis by touch alone. What is touch adding to your understanding? Compare your analysis against how the perfume/cologne is advertised in its print ad.

LEVEL UP

Free Tool

To help you share and analyze tactile products, we recommend you use Google Slides.

Tool	URL	Description
Google Slides	In Google Drive, click on "New" and choose "Google Slides." Students may copy our template: https://bit.ly/designforcomposition-slidetemplate	Google Slides is a synchronous, collaborative slide-design platform. It allows you to create shareable slideshows and comment on features of the slideshow.

Learn More

In the section below, learn more about how designers are creative with the elements of touch. Several sources feature examples based on productions or research.

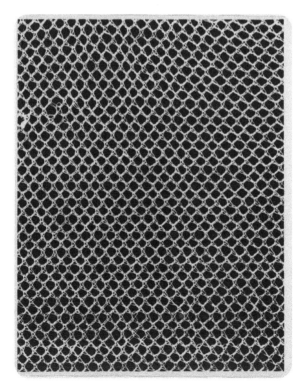

Figure 3: Art Sinsabaugh, Texture Study, Student Project, Institute of Design, Chicago Illinois (late 1940s).

Texture

Texture is described as the surface quality or feel of an object (or the appearance of surface quality and feel in 2D graphic design). Two types of texture include tactile and visual. The variation of light and dark patterns can create visual texture. Texture is the surface of an object.

Interiors + Sources explores the role of texture in surface design of products, but these goals of texture (pattern of texture, gloss of texture, depth of texture, touch of texture) might be applied to product design: https://bit.ly/designforcomposition32. In art, texture has been used, like product design, to evoke emotion and communicate. Read about how artists use texture to create "tactile portraits for the blind": https://bit.ly/designforcomposition-tactile.

Form/Shape

Cornell University describes the planned or strategic arrangement of form and shape in two-dimensional and three-dimensional space. In this chapter, you should focus on form and shape as they pertain to what is happening in three-dimensional design of forms and shapes. These forms or shapes can be geometric or organic (shapes inspired by the natural environment) to suggest ideas or evoke feelings: https://bit.ly/designforcomposition33.

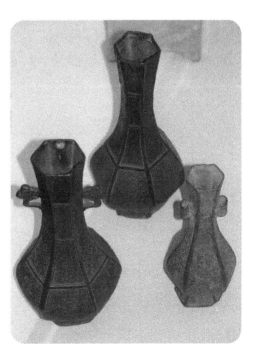

Figure 4 (left): Organic Vase, courtesy of Flickr Commons.

Figure 5 (right): Bronze Alter Vase with hexagonal sections from Yuan Dynasty (13th - 14th Century), courtesy of the British Museum.

Mass/Volume

In the three-dimensional world of product design, mass is no longer the "perceived weight" but actual feel of the weight and depth with which we interact. The mass or bulk of the three-dimensional work is often discussed in art such as sculptures and in architecture. One might argue that product design does consider many of the elements of sculpture, including mass, to achieve its aesthetic effect and deliver its message: https://bit.ly/designforcomposition34.

Figure 6: Tullio Sabas, Prototype of Video Telephone, courtesy of Flickr Commons.

CHAPTER THREE: BLIND TOUCH

CREATIVE PROJECT

Blind Touch Test in Product Design

BEFORE YOU BEGIN

Understand common elements of design as they might relate to users' experience of touch: texture, shape, and mass. We recommend that you read the description and examples of these elements under the "Learn More" section of this chapter.

Total Estimated Time

- 30 minutes for finding product
- 30 minutes for Creativity: Doing
- 30 minutes for Creativity: Sharing

Skills: Identify tactile elements (texture, shape, and mass), recognizing creativity in the application of these elements in perfume or cologne.

Sharing Options: Depending on how your class or group is asked to deliver this project, you may be sharing the work virtually or in person.

Synchronous/Asynchronous: This activity can be conducted both synchronously and asynchronously with some modification.

For live activity (in person or synchronous), we recommend that you work with a group to analyze found perfume or cologne using presentation software like Google Slides or another platform that your instructor identifies.

For asynchronous interactions with your class or group, we recommend substituting the group exchange of product with your individual recording of a touch test. Please refer to the steps under Creativity: Doing.

I. CREATIVITY: DOING

Overview

The objective of this activity is to explore the ways tactile (or touch) elements of design contribute to the message or ideas suggested by an everyday product and what it says about who it is targeting (audience). By feeling and not seeing, you might gain insight into how designers thought the tactile design of products might contribute to how you think and feel about the product (experience/use, value, appeal to audience). Here are step-by-step directions for what to do in the classroom and what to do at home.

Directions for Live (In-Person) Activity

1. **Selecting and Bagging a Bottle [outside class]**: Choose one cologne or perfume bottle [without the package]. We recommend that you choose a bottle with distinct textures, shapes, or mass. Each student will bring the bottle in an unmarked brown bag and place it on a designated table at the start of class.

2. **Form Groups**: Your instructor may decide how to form your groups. We recommend a small group (ideally 3-4 students each). Each group should pick one bag from the table to analyze.

3. **Blind Touch Test**: Each student takes a turn reaching into the bag to feel the item and note texture, shape, and mass.

4. **Answer questions in the inventory table**: Use the three inventory tables on the next page (texture, shape, and mass) or create a copy of the template in Google Slides and use it for sharing later: https://tinyurl.com/DFC-Ch3-Inventory.

5. **Reveal**: Reveal the cologne bottle to your small group to discuss what you accurately observed and described compared to the reality of seeing the bottle, specifically focusing on texture, shape, and mass.

6. **Fill out a table of questions in the template** describing the bottle.

Directions for Asynchronous Activity

1. **Select a bottle**: Choose one cologne or perfume bottle [without the package]. We recommend choosing a bottle with distinct textures, shapes, or mass.
2. **Touch Test**: You'll be focusing on describing in words how you feel the item and note the texture, shape, and mass.
3. **Answer questions in the inventory table**: Use the three inventory tables on the next page (texture, shape, and mass) or create a copy of the template in Google Slides and use it for sharing later: https://tinyurl.com/DFC-Ch3-Inventory.

These tables will guide you in the tactile analysis of product design.

Tactile Analysis of Product Design: Texture	
Type of Touch: Texture	Describe your sensory experience (by touch) in terms of **texture**.
Design for Value, Experience, or Use	Describe how the **texture** of the product impacts your sense of the value, experience of the product.
Design for Audience Appeal	Who do you think is the target audience? Is the perfume/cologne bottle targeting male or female? Is it gender neutral? How does **texture** of the product help you determine this audience?

Tactile Analysis of Product Design: Shape	
Type of Touch: Shape	Describe your sensory experience (by touch) in terms of **shape**.
Design for Value, Experience, or Use	Describe how the **shape** of the product impacts your sense of the value, experience of the product.
Design for Audience Appeal	Describe how the **shape** of the product impacts its appeal to an audience.

Tactile Analysis of Product Design: Mass	
Type of Touch: Mass	Describe your sensory experience (by touch) in terms of **mass**.
Design for Value, Experience, or Use	Describe how the **texture** of the product impacts your sense of the value, experience of the product. For perfume bottles, you might consider mass in terms of how it might fill up in the hand.
Design for Audience Appeal	Describe how the **mass** of the product impacts its appeal to an audience.

Tactile Analysis of Product Design: Texture

Type of Touch: Texture

Design for Value, Experience, or Use

Design for Audience Appeal

Tactile Analysis of Product Design: Shape

Type of Touch: Shape

Design for Value, Experience, or Use

Design for Audience Appeal

Tactile Analysis of Product Design: Mass

Type of Touch: Mass	
Design for Value, Experience, or Use	
Design for Audience Appeal	

II. CREATIVITY: REFLECTING

Reflection is an important metacognitive process of learning because it helps you recall and identify ideas and concepts you learned and articulate how you understand them. You may be asked to provide an oral or written reflection in response to the following questions, either virtually or in person. If you are in a team, work with your team members to answer the questions below.

Questions for Live (In-Person) Activity

- Were you able to identify the target audience of the bottle of cologne or perfume (whether it was meant for a man or woman)?
- How did texture, mass, and shape together help you determine the audience?
- Did you rely on one feature more than another?
- Why do you think that product designers emphasized that feature for the target audience?
- Do you think it was a "creative" feature? Why or why not?

Questions for Online/Individual Activity

- How did texture, mass, and shape together help you determine the audience?
- Did one feature point to the target audience more than another?
- Why do you think that product designers emphasized that feature for the target audience?
- Do you think it was a "creative" feature (why or why not?)

SPEAKING
APPLICATION
VOCAL EXPRESSION

"A voice is a human gift; it should be cherished and used, to utter fully human speech as possible." — Margaret Atwood

SET THE SCENE

Vocalics or vocal expression is the study of how voice is modulated to contribute to nonverbal communication (communication that goes with or without words). For instance, the pitch, rate, volume, articulation, pronunciation, and even silence contribute to how we might interpret the spoken words of Martin Luther King, Jr. Or consider how you say "Hello." Your word might be read to convey not just salutary greeting but your mood, attitude, and feeling at the moment. It might be spoken grudgingly or willingly. It might project flirtation or friendliness. This chapter helps you become more aware of how vocalics communicates meaning. Ultimately, improving your awareness of vocalics can help you improve your performance in a variety of orally-based communication projects in the future (from presentations to audio recordings).

Figure 1: Martin Luther King, Jr. speaking at a news conference in New York City on November 5, 1964.

CONNECT TO CREATIVITY

Chapter 4 asks students to listen to several readings of a classic poem. After studying the vocalics, you will be asked to read it yourself, analyzing the vocalics in your own reading. Comparing vocalics, you will increase your awareness of how vocalics carry personality, emotion, and feeling.

Figure 2: Boy singing in a microphone. Courtesy of unsplash.com.

By completing this activity, you will

- **Explore** how voice carries distinct "personality" profiles or mood attributes.
- **Analyze and apply** vocalics strategy.
- **Reflect** on your choices in vocalics subject and application.

LEVEL UP

Free Tools

Part of the assignment is to record yourself applying vocalics, so that it can be shared and analyzed by the class. Because the performance focuses on vocalics, the visual component is not necessary. The following is a list of free tools that you can use:

Tool	URL	Description
ScreenPal	https://screenpal.com/	Free to create and share. Screen only for the free version.
Quicktime	https://support.apple.com/downloads/quicktime	Free for Macs or PC; Records video and audio. You can choose to record only in audio.
HAHAmoji	Download for free in iOS and Android. In the Apple App Store, look up "HAHAmoji." For Android, visit: https://bit.ly/designforcomposition-hahamoji.	Animate your face in a smartphone using an emoji to help work on facial expressions as you try your vocalics (think of it as using an animated "mask").
Bitmoji	https://www.bitmoji.com/	Free and send to anyone in any app; computers also (Chrome).
Camera App	Smartphone	Free
Voice Memo App	Smartphone	Free

Learn More

You'll find more design perspectives than you could ever wish for available freely on the web. Many of these sources offer good advice based on experience and even, at times, research. Some of them are not as reliable. We've distilled these sites into some of the best available for you as you begin your design work. You might find these samples and perspectives inspiring.

Listen to an example of vocalics employed by Actor Benedict Cumberbatch: https://bit.ly/designforcomposition41. Cumberbatch provides a performance where our reception of the content ("I'm a little teapot" song familiar to preschoolers) is altered by vocalics (tone, pausing, even body language).

CREATIVE PROJECT

Vocal Expression

BEFORE YOU BEGIN

Watch "Benedict Cumberbatch perform 'I'm a Little Teapot'" to better understand vocalics. How does he use his voice to dramatize the nursery song? For instance, where does he pause? Where does he speed up? And to what effect?

Group Activity: Up to three participants.

Total Estimated Time: 1.5 hours for Doing and Reflecting.

Skills: Application of creativity through vocalics, understanding of vocalics and its impact on meaning and interpretation.

(Optional) Sharing: Your instructors may ask you to share your recording online through Tumblr, Wordpress, or your course management system.

I. CREATIVITY: DOING

"Did you know that the human voice is the only pure instrument? That it has notes no other instrument has?" — Nina Simone

Overview

This exercise has two parts (Part A and B). First, you will practice analyzing vocalics by studying two readings of a famous poem. Then you will apply what you've identified through your own recording of the poem using tools we've suggested. The goal of this project is to explore the impact of vocalics on meaning and make you more aware of how you apply vocalics in any speech!

Directions for Practice

(Approximately 30 minutes)

1. **Read** the first stanza of the poem "Raven" to yourself.

2. **Select one of the readings**: One group of students (about half of the class) should listen to one reading of the poem (James Earl Jones). The second group of students (about the other half of the class) should listen to the other (Simpsons).

3. **Identify by annotating the five elements of vocalics for each reader**: pitch, rate, volume, pronunciation, and fillers/silence listed in the table below and mark up the poem in the space provided. Groups may want to listen several times to identify different applications of vocalics.

4. **Discuss** results in small groups or as class.

"RAVEN" BY EDGAR ALLEN POE

Once upon a midnight dreary, while I pondered, weak and weary,
Over many a quaint and curious volume of forgotten lore—
      While I nodded, nearly napping, suddenly there came a tapping,
As of some one gently rapping, rapping at my chamber door.
"'Tis some visitor," I muttered, "tapping at my chamber door—
      Only this and nothing more."

https://bit.ly/designforcomposition42

After listening to this reading of the poem, follow the directions provided and mark up the stanza below according to the use of vocalics.

Directions

Vocalic Attributes	Definition	Your Interpretation
Volume	Volume is the loudness of the speaker.	**Underline** words where the speaker seems to speak louder or softer.
Rate or speed	Rate is the speed of speaking in words per minute from slow to fast.	**Circle** areas where the speaker speeds up or slows down.
Pronunciation (accents, emphasis)	Pronunciation is the way in which a word is pronounced.	**Mark a "P"** over words where the speaker places a special emphasis or pronounces a word in a different/unusual way.
Fillers, pauses, silence	Fillers are extraneous sounds (such as "um"); pauses can be used to communicate a dramatic moment, hesitancy, etc.	**Highlight** fillers that appear or pauses or dramatic breaks in speaking.

Once upon a midnight dreary, while I pondered, weak and weary,
Over many a quaint and curious volume of forgotten lore—
    While I nodded, nearly napping, suddenly there came a tapping,
As of some one gently rapping, rapping at my chamber door.
"'Tis some visitor," I muttered, "tapping at my chamber door—
    Only this and nothing more."

https://bit.ly/designforcomposition43

After listening to this reading of the poem, follow the directions provided and mark up the stanza below according to the use of vocalics.

Directions

Vocalic Attributes	Definition	Your Interpretation
Volume	Volume is the loudness of the speaker.	**Underline** words where the speaker seems to speak louder or softer.
Rate or speed	Rate is the speed of speaking in words per minute from slow to fast.	**Circle** areas where the speaker speeds up or slows down.
Pronunciation (accents, emphasis)	Pronunciation is the way in which a word is pronounced.	**Mark a "P"** over words where the speaker places a special emphasis or pronounces a word in a different/unusual way.
Fillers, pauses, silence	Fillers are extraneous sounds (such as "um"); pauses can be used to communicate a dramatic moment, hesitancy, etc.	**Highlight** fillers that appear or pauses or dramatic breaks in speaking.

Once upon a midnight dreary, while I pondered, weak and weary,
Over many a quaint and curious volume of forgotten lore—
        While I nodded, nearly napping, suddenly there came a tapping,
As of some one gently rapping, rapping at my chamber door.
"'Tis some visitor," I muttered, "tapping at my chamber door—
        Only this and nothing more."

PROJECT 4

Directions for Creative Application

(Approximately 30 minutes)

1. **Read** the first stanza of the poem "Raven" to yourself again.
2. **Write out AND annotate on the poem how you might apply the five elements of vocalics**: here's an additional challenge —you must select an audience (to Preschoolers or serious fans of Edgar Allan Poe).
3. **Record** your application using free tools suggested in this chapter.

Your Reading		
Audience		
Directions		
Vocalic Attributes	Definition	Your Interpretation
Volume	Volume is the loudness of the speaker.	**Underline** words where the speaker seems to speak louder or softer.
Rate or speed	Rate is the speed of speaking in words per minute from slow to fast.	**Circle** areas where the speaker speeds up or slows down.
Pronunciation (accents, emphasis)	Pronunciation is the way in which a word is pronounced.	**Mark a "P"** over words where the speaker places a special emphasis or pronounces a word in a different/ unusual way.
Fillers, pauses, silence	Fillers are extraneous sounds (such as "um"); pauses can be used to communicate a dramatic moment, hesitancy, etc.	**Highlight** fillers that appear or pauses or dramatic breaks in speaking.

Once upon a midnight dreary, while I pondered, weak and weary,
Over many a quaint and curious volume of forgotten lore—
　　　While I nodded, nearly napping, suddenly there came a tapping,
As of some one gently rapping, rapping at my chamber door.
"'Tis some visitor," I muttered, "tapping at my chamber door—
　　　Only this and nothing more."

II. CREATIVITY: REFLECTING

Oral Reflection: Peer Feedback

(Approximately 15 minutes)

Depending on how much time you have in class, instructors may ask you to provide oral or written reflection. Here are some questions you can ask your peer(s):

- What elements of vocalics stood out for you in the reading that helped you understand or enjoy the poem?
- How did volume, rate or speed, pronunciation, or fillers adjust or change in the reading?
- How might applying a similar process of annotating vocalics alter the way you perform a future presentation?

5 INTERACTING APPLICATION THINKING/ RETHINKING APP ICONS FOR AN EVERYDAY ACTIVITY

"Design is thinking made visual." — Saul Bass

SET THE SCENE

Mobile devices such as cell phones, tablets, and laptops now include applications (often referred to as "apps") that are downloadable and accessible within moments. An app is designed as a user-friendly shortcut, often a visual, for accessing and then launching a program. We can search for or identify apps to serve different purposes, solve problems, make tasks easier (or more efficient), or communicate in certain ways. App icons convey a large amount of information, and perform a variety of functions, in a small amount of space, often a square inch or less on the screen of your device. They are highly visual and, if designed well, memorable or representative of the activity they are intended to perform. The icon could also bring attention to how one might feel about the activity and interact with it, such as the logo in Figure 1.

Well-designed apps are easy to recall and find on your device quickly. While we often remember the look of most commonly used apps, such as the bird on Twitter or "f" of Facebook, we often navigate these graphical interfaces intuitively and without a great deal of thought given to their design, layout, or visual appeal. What makes an app icon memorable? What makes an app usable? This chapter gives you an opportunity to think/rethink multiple designs of an app icon.

Figure 1 (left): Icon showing activity.

Figure 2 (below): Memorable app icons

CONNECT TO CREATIVITY

Chapter 5 invites you to explore making visually compact and memorable symbols. This activity will help you recognize creativity and why careful rethinking may be required to create symbols that convey ideas succinctly and tell their story. While you may not create actual apps yourself, you may find it helpful to create symbols that are similar to represent processes and concepts in presentations or posters.

This chapter exercises your creative skills in the following ways:

- **Distill** an everyday activity to an essential concept, develop key word(s).
- **Think/rethink** multiple versions of the concept with prototypes that are modifying or combining at least two noun project icons and playing with color.
- **Creatively learn to use** the Picture Format Tool.
- **Share** your app design and see if the class can guess the concept.

LEVEL UP

Free Tools

Designers can find hundreds of freely available tools on the web. We've assembled some of the top free sites for you here. Use these sites as a starting point to identify fonts for use in this design project.

Tool	URL	Description
Picture Format Tool	Available through PowerPoint or Microsoft Word. Office 365 is FREE. https://www.microsoft.com/en-us/education/products/office	After you drag and drop an image or icon, click on the visual and the picture format tool appears at the top of the document as one of your tools. Picture format allows you to remove background; make "corrections" to the brightness or contrast; add/change color; add artistic effects; change transparency, etc. You can layer multiple images and combine them to make your own distinct icon.
Noun Project	https://thenounproject.com/	"Icons and Photos for Everything," with the aim of creating a global visual language that unites.

Learn More

You'll find more design perspectives than you could ever wish for available freely on the web. Many of these sources offer good advice based on experience and even, at times, research. Some of them are not as reliable. We've distilled these sites into some of the best available for you as you begin your design work. You might find these samples and perspectives inspiring.

Aaron Draplin, "Aaron Draplin Takes on a Logo Design Challenge," YouTube Video, 16 min. Graphic designer AaronDraplin walks through the process of making a logo. He starts with the brainstorming process (writing out the name of the logo) or what he calls "sketching:" https://bit.ly/designforcomposition51.

CREATIVE PROJECT

App Logo for an Everyday Activity

BEFORE YOU BEGIN

Watch Aaron Draplin in "Aaron Draplin Takes on a Logo Design Challenge" to understand the design process from a designer's perspective to get a design that is unique. It's all about exploring, sketching, and thinking/rethinking multiple ideas and versions!

Group Activity: Up to three participants.

Total Estimated Time: 1 hour for Design Doing; Design Reflecting.

Skills: Discovery process, multiple prototyping, visual design application.

Sharing Options: Your instructor may want you to share your App Logo and feedback virtually or in person.

Synchronous/Asynchronous: This activity can be conducted both synchronously and asynchronously.

For live activity (in person or synchronous), we recommend that you share your project by exchanging the icon. Listen carefully to the response without interruption and take notes. The following are questions you can ask your peers or teammates (without telling them what activity the icon represents!).

For asynchronous activity, we recommend that the icons and questions be answered on a blog or other multimedia sharing platforms such as VoiceThread.

I. CREATIVITY: DOING

"Design is a plan for arranging elements in such a way as best to accomplish a particular purpose." — Charles Eames

Overview

Creatively design an app icon using only typeface and graphic design. In this challenge, you'll explore an important aspect of creativity—prototyping and testing the versions with your peers.

Directions for Choosing an App Idea

1. **Choose an app idea for an everyday activity**—something that people don't already have in a smartphone or tablet.
2. **Select** one everyday activity that might be reflected in an app.
3. **List** three attributes for that activity.

Directions for Creating a Logo/Icon

4. **Create a "logo" or icon** for your chosen app.
5. **Select** images from the Noun Project that might reflect that attribute effectively.
6. **Design** three versions of the icon using the images from the Noun Project.
7. **Use** Word's picture format tool to remove background, change colors, and combine images.

Sample App Logo	
Everyday Activity	Daily Journaling
Attributes to Your Everday Activity	
1	"Daily" (Reflect a day)
2	Writing instrument for journaling (pen or pencil)
3	Pad on which one writes

Four Icons from The Noun Project

 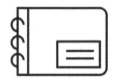

Final App (3 Versions)

MS Word's "Picture Format" tool: Remove background, add different colors, combine images together

Your App Logo	
Everyday Activity	

Attributes to Your Everday Activity

1	
2	
3	

Four Icons from The Noun Project

Final App (3 Versions)

MS Word's "Picture Format" tool: Remove background, add different colors, combine images together

CHAPTER FIVE: RETHINKING APPS 81

II. CREATIVITY: REFLECTING

Oral Reflection: Peer Feedback

Reflection is an important metacognitive process of learning because it helps you recall and identify ideas and concepts you learned and articulate how you understand them. You may be asked to provide an oral or written reflection in response to the following questions, either virtually or in person. If you are in a team, work with your team members to answer the questions below.

Questions for Peers/Teammates

- What activity or concept do these icons represent?
- Which version of the icon best represent the activity or concept? Why?
- Could parts of one prototype or a combination of these prototypes improve the communication of the activity? If so, which?

Written Reflection: Individual Response

Write a paragraph in response to the following questions. Support your ideas by providing concrete references to your experience in the exercise:

Questions for Self/Individual

- What did you enjoy most about designing your icon? What was the most challenging?
- How did making multiple versions of your icon help with developing a creative icon?
- If you had more time, what would you do to enhance creativity in your icon?

6 TOUCHING
EVALUATION
CREATIVITY IN
CLOTHING AND
TEXTURE

"Design is not just what it looks like and feels like. Design is how it works." — Steve Jobs

SET THE SCENE

In the context of product design, texture is the feel (tactile characteristics) and look of something on its surface. These surfaces could be on everyday items that we interact with, such as pencils, cups, paper, computers, brushes, bags, towels, etc. We talk about texture in the way we describe the feel and look of furniture and aspects of architecture, such as glass, buildings, and floors. Visual and tactile characteristics are essential in the design of clothing fabric in particular because the look and feel of fabric carries with it various kinds of social meaning/ standing in different contexts and different communities: a glossy silk evening dress is appropriate at a formal event but not for a meeting with a school administrator; a studded leather jacket and rough jeans may be appropriate for a rock concert but not for a job interview. Fabric (and clothing) sometimes carry a message about the personality of the wearer at the moment: elegant, eccentric, sporty, casual, romantic, down-to-earth, fun, playful, serious, rebellious, approachable, tough, feminine, masculine, etc. In this chapter, we will explore how we might identify texture that is creative. What makes certain texture more creative than others? How does creative texture impact the social messages carried in the design of clothing? We'll explore these ideas in this chapter by developing a rubric for creative use of texture.

CONNECT TO CREATIVITY

Chapter 6 asks you to investigate the connection between visual and tactile texture and how they communicate creatively. The goal of this lesson is to understand strategies for evaluating creative use of texture and what the creative use of texture communicates. This chapter allows you to evaluate creativity in the design of fabric as well as in the wearer's usage in two parts. In part one, you will generate a rubric. In part two, you will apply it to a specific item of clothing that you think is "creative" (See *Learn More*).

This chapter exercises your creative skills in the following ways:

- **Learn about** basic categories of visual and tactile texture in fabric.
- **Explore** how visual and tactile textures may communicate.
- **Generate** a rubric of the creative use of texture.
- **Apply** the rubric to a creative item of clothing.

LEVEL UP

Learn More

As you explore texture in fabrics and items you encounter in your daily life, you'll find a variety of tools available for you to archive what you find. In addition, you'll find a variety of sites that will help you think in different ways about texture. For example, try What is Fabric Texture and Why Should I Care? https://bit.ly/designforcomposition61.

Basic Categories for Texture

Visual Texture: There are four basic visual motifs or units of textile design.

1. **Geometric Motifs:** Patterns in geometric shapes
2. **Realistic Motifs:** Patterns of natural or man-made objects
3. **Stylized Motifs:** Patterns of natural or man-made objects that are less recognizable
4. **Abstract Motifs:** Patterns of color, shape, or size that are not connected to natural or man-made objects

Figure 1: Example of geometric motif. Mantle cloth (wool). AD 600-800. Wari, Peru.

Figure 2: Example of realistic motif. Uchishiki (Altar Cloth). Edo period (1615-1868), Japan. Art Institute Chicago. Gift of Martin A. Ryerson.

Figure 3: Example of stylized motif. Bedcover (Roses and Buds Quilt). Harriet Wilson Curtis (Maker). C. 1908. Art Institute Chicago. Gift of Helen E. Bournique and Mrs. Frank A. Friebe.

Figure 4: Example of abstract motif. Textile fragment. A.D. 900. Chiquerillo, Palpa Valley, Peru. Art Institute Chicago. Gift of Alan R. Sawyer.

Tactile Texture: As noted earlier, weaves of fabric and its texture impact how the cloth feels against your skin as well as how it looks. Silk fabric is a good example of fabric that is often selected in clothing for several reasons, particularly because it has a distinctive feel and look: fine silk weave has a soft, smooth, glossy texture but it is also light. Basic types of how we feel fabric may fall under these three areas:

1. **Surface Texture:** Smooth/fluid/shiny to rough/dull (includes woolly, fuzzy, bumpy)
2. **Pressure Texture:** Softness (includes flexible) to hardness (includes plasticity)
3. **Weight Texture:** Lightness to heaviness

Figure 5: Example of surface texture. Feathered tunic. 1470/1532. Chimu, Peru. Art Institute Chicago. Kate S. Buckingham Endowment.

Figure 6: Example of pressure texture. French gaming bag (silk over leather). 1675-1700. Art Institute Chicago. Gift of Mrs. John N. Jewett through the Antiquarian Society.

Figure 7: Example of weight texture. Veil with Russian Imperial Family Coat of Arms (cotton). 1875-1900. Belgium. Art Institute Chicago. Gift of Mrs. Potter Palmer, Sr. through the Antiquarian Society.

CHAPTER SIX: CLOTHING & TEXTURE

CREATIVE PROJECT

Evaluate Creativity in Clothing and Texture

BEFORE YOU BEGIN

Each student should find one item of clothing that uses texture creatively. Students should read/reread "Categories of Texture" in this chapter.

Group Activity: Up to three participants.

Total Estimated Time: 1.5 hours for Design Doing and Design Reflecting.

Skills: Evaluation process.

Sharing Options: Your instructor may wish you to share your project and feedback virtually or in person.

Synchronous/Asynchronous: This activity can be conducted both synchronously and asynchronously.

For live activity (in person or synchronous), we recommend that you share your project in teams/groups for part one (generating the attributes of creative texture) and then work in smaller teams to apply the rubric to a creatively textured fabric.

For asynchronous activity, we recommend that you work on part one (generating the attributes of creative texture) on a shared Google Doc; you might also create your individual rubric on a blog. You will then apply the rubric to a creatively textured fabric.

Figure 8 (left): Creative visual texture example. Vivienne Westwood. Man's ensemble (Jacket, Shirt, Trousers, Shoes, and Cuff Links). England, London, Spring/Summer 2014. LACHMA.

Figure 9 (right): Creative tactile texture example. Gucci. Man's Shirt (leather). Italy, Florence, 1973. LACHMA.

I. CREATIVITY: DOING

"Look at usual things with unusual eyes." — *Vico Magistretti*

Overview

Develop a creativity rubric focusing on the categories of visual texture and tactile texture. Apply the rubric to an item of clothing. In this challenge, you'll explore an important aspect of creativity —texture and design.

Directions for Brainstorming

1. **Brainstorm** attributes of the "creative" use of texture in fabric in the two categories (visual and tactile) in small groups or teams.
2. **Share** the results as classmates or group members.
3. **Decide** what attributes are most prominent and provide a rationale
4. **Organize** attributes and be prepared to use them for part two.

Sample Rubric: Visual Texture	
Visual Texture	**What attributes are common in really creative uses of visual texture?** When considering general creative attributes of visual texture, review the list of basic visual texture types and think about creative visual textures that you've seen. **What makes visual texture stand out or look unique? How does it draw your attention? Is it how it is graphically applied on the clothing (location, size/proportion, color, etc.)?** After identifying the attribute, provide a brief rationale and example.

#	General Creative Attributes	Rationale
Ex.	Motifs used in unusual ways on clothes—such as optical illusions	Unusual or surprising use of visual motifs draw attention. Example: Trompe-L'Oeil drawings on t-shirts

Sample Rubric: Tactile Texture

Tactile Texture	What attributes are common in creative tactile textures (surface, touch, weight)? When considering general creative attributes of tactile texture, review the list of basic tactile texture types. What makes certain tactile attributes unique or memorable on clothing? Identify in the fields below creative attributes of the tactile texture types, along with a brief rationale and example.

#	General Creative Attributes	Rationale
Ex.	Weight texture feels different from what's expected	Having weight texture runs contrary to what is expected, makes it interesting and unusual for the wearer (and perhaps observer). Example: "Leather" textured fabric that is actually light rather than heavy

Your Rubric: Visual Texture

Visual Texture	What attributes are common in really creative uses of visual texture? When considering general creative attributes of visual texture, review the list of basic visual texture types and think about creative visual textures that you've seen. What makes visual texture stand out or look unique? How does it draw your attention? Is it how it is graphically applied on the clothing (location, size/proportion, color, etc.)? After identifying the attribute, provide a brief rationale and example.

#	General Creative Attributes	Rationale
1		
2		
3		

Tactile Texture	What attributes are common in creative tactile textures (surface, touch, weight)? When considering general creative attributes of tactile texture, review the list of basic tactile texture types. What makes certain tactile attributes unique or memorable on clothing? Identify in the fields below creative attributes of the tactile texture types, along with a brief rationale and example.

#	General Creative Attributes	Rationale
1		
2		
3		

Directions for Analyzing Texture

Steps for Live (In-Person) Activity	
Select	**In a team or group, select** one item of clothing to analyze using the rubric.
Agree	**As a team, agree upon** a component of a visual and tactile texture of fabric in a specific item of clothing that you think is "creative." (See **Learn More**.)
Assess	**Assess** to what degree components of texture (visual, tactile) are creatively used based on the rubric. What does that creative texture communicate?
Reflect	**Reflect**: Share your assessments of a piece of creative clothing. Does the rubric work? What needs to be changed or adjusted?

PROJECT 6

Steps for Asynchronous Activity

Select	**Select** one item of clothing to analyze using the rubric.
Identify	**Identify** a component of a visual and tactile texture of fabric in a specific item of clothing that you think is "creative." (See **Learn More**.)
Assess	**Assess** to what degree components of texture (visual, tactile) are creatively used based on the rubric. What does that creative texture communicate?
Reflect	**Reflect**: Share your assessments of a piece of creative clothing. Does the rubric work? What needs to be changed or adjusted?

1. **Select** one item of clothing that features a creative visual and/or tactile texture to analyze.

2. **Assess** the basic components of visual or tactile texture of clothing (see the table "Assessment of Texture"). What texture seems to meet the criteria listed in the rubric? Explain how or why. Are there aspects of the clothing

Assessment of Texture

Item	Type of clothing		
Overall Texture Description			

Criteria	Description of Texture	To what degree is the texture creative?	From your perpective, what does that creative texture communicate about the "personality" of the wearer? How might this perception of texture reflect a person's community?
Visual Texture (geometric, realistic, stylized, abstract or none—solid color)			
Other aspects of visual texture?			
Tactile Texture (surface, pressure, weight)			
Other aspects of tactile texture?			

II. CREATIVITY: REFLECTING

Oral Reflection: Peer Feedback

Provide feedback by exchanging the item, attributes, and rubric among groups. If working asynchronously, post your own reflection to these answers. Read and respond to the posts of others. The following are questions you can ask your peer(s):

Questions for Peers/Teammates

- What does the texture feel like?
- How do the attributes help your understanding of of what texture communicates?
- How or in what ways is the texture of the item creative? Were there attributes of texture that were not listed in the rubric? If so, how would you modify the rubric?
- How does the rubric allow you to be more critical about evaluating the creativity of texture?

Written Reflection: Individual Response

Write a paragraph in response to the following questions. Support your ideas by providing concrete references to your experience in the exercise:

Questions for Self/Individual

- What did you learn about texture through this process?
- How did designing the rubric help you think about creative uses or applications of texture?

7 SPEAKING AND WRITING APPLICATION
VENTRILOQUY AND RHETORICAL DEVICES

"It usually takes more than three weeks to prepare a good impromptu speech."
— Mark Twain

SET THE SCENE

How did great speeches get to be great speeches? Some of it is timing. Some of it comes from the speaker, how they said it, and what they said. Regardless of timing, style, or content, great speeches require practice; and even better speeches pay attention to language. The practice of modeling one's speech after sample addresses is one of the classic ways you can pay attention to how you speak (vocalics) and how you phrase the speech (use of rhetorical devices in oral language). In this chapter, you'll be working on both.

Figure 1: njTare. Drawing of Martin Luther King, Jr. writing. Courtesy of Flickr. Licensed under Creative Commons.

CONNECT TO CREATIVITY

Ventriloquy ("speak from the stomach"; venter "belly" + loqui "speak") is the act of throwing one's voice so that it appears the voice is comes from elsewhere. In Chapter 7, you will creatively explore how you can learn from speech models through "ventriloquy" —that is, by throwing your "voice" into a great speech to explore speech style and the art of using rhetorical devices.

Figure 2: Adrien Coquet. Noun Project.

By working on this activity, you will

- **Understand and identify** the effect of some common rhetorical devices
- **Identify** one or two specific rhetorical devices in a famous speech (selected by an individual or team)
- **Creatively apply** one or two rhetorical devices in your ventriloquy (individual work)
- **Reflect** on your choices (and the choices of others, if working in a team)

LEVEL UP

Learn More

Nancy Duarte. "16 Rhetorical Devices That Will Make You Sound like Steve Jobs." https://bit.ly/designforcomposition71.

Silva Rhetoricae. Learn more about different types of rhetorical devices. Read how these devices work in classic works of literature and think about ways you might incorporate these devices into your own speech. Visit Silva Rhetoricae: http://rhetoric.byu.edu/.

Rhetorical Devices of Repetition and Word Order: Deliberate design of words for repetition, order, effect, and address are called rhetorical devices. The following are some common rhetorical devices that you'll see in everyday advertising, but you'll also see them in speeches, writing, and other forms of communication.

Repetition		
Type	**Definition**	**Example**
Alliteration	repetition of the same sound beginning several words in sequence	"**S**top playing games. **S**tart playing guitar." — Sparrow Guitar ad
Anadiplosis	repetition of the last word (or phrase) from the previous line, clause, or sentence at the beginning of the next	"Office suite with **bedroom**? Or **bedroom** suite with office?" — SpringHill Suites ad
Anaphora	repetition of a word or phrase at the beginning of successive phrases, clauses or lines	"**Choose** Sony. **Choose** Wisely." — Sony tagline
Epistrophe	repetition of the same word or phrase at the end of successive phrases, clauses, or sentences	"The Roman **Empire**. The British **Empire**. The Fedex **Empire**. Nothing lasts forever." — DHL shipping ad

Word Order		
Type	**Definition**	**Example**
Antithesis	opposition or contrast of ideas or words in a balanced or parallel construction	"It's an **arrival**. It's a **departure**." — Acura car ad
Climax	cumulative arrangement of words, phrases or clauses in an order of ascending power; often the emphatic word in one phrase or clause is repeated as the first emphatic word of the next	"Dreams are **good**. Realities are **better**." — Citibank ad

CREATIVE PROJECT

Ventriloquy and Rhetorical Devices

BEFORE YOU BEGIN

Review the selection of Rhetorical Devices that we've provided and also read Nancy Duarte's short article.

Group Activity: Up to three participants.

Total Estimated Time: 1 hour for Doing and Reflecting.

Skills: Application of creativity through the use of rhetorical devices and your "ventriloquy." Through this practice, you will gain a better understanding of rhetorical devices and its impact on great speeches.

Sharing Options: Depending on how your class or group is asked to deliver this project, you may be sharing the work virtually on a blog or in person.

Synchronous/Asynchronous: This activity can be conducted both synchronously and asynchronously.

I. CREATIVITY: DOING

"Take chances, make mistakes. That's how you grow." — Mary Tyler Moore

Steps for Live (In-Person) Activity

Modeling (15 mins.)

1. Select a speech from American Rhetoric (Top 100 Speeches): https://www. americanrhetoric.com/newtop100speeches.htm.
2. Paste at least one significant paragraph to a PowerPoint or Google Slide.
3. Highlight and name rhetorical devices you recognize from our list.

Practice (15 mins.)

1. Select a topic of your choice
2. Use your topic in the speech you selected from American Rhetoric. Try to keep the devices and the style.

Discuss and Share (20 mins.)

1. Read both the original and the ventriloquized piece to the rest of the class.

2. Classmates or group members should identify: A) speech and speaker, B) rhetorical devices in the original, and C) topic applied.

Steps for Asynchronous Activity

Modeling (15 mins.)

1. Select a speech from American Rhetoric (Top 100 Speeches): https://www.americanrhetoric.com/newtop100speeches.htm.

2. Paste at least one significant paragraph to a Google Slide.

3. Highlight and name rhetorical devices you recognize from our list of six rhetorical devices provided in this chapter.

Practice (15 mins.)

1. Select a topic of your choice

2. Use your topic in the speech you selected from American Rhetoric. Try to keep the devices and the style!

Discuss and Share (20 mins.)

1. Read both the original and the ventriloquized piece. Record your reading via video on the device of your choosing.

2. Classmates or group members should identify: A) speech and speaker, B) rhetorical devices in the original, C) topic applied.

3. Classmates or group members should post their responses via the course discussion board.

PROJECT 7

Topic: Mandatory Use of Bike Helmets at a University
Speech: Malcolm X, Ballot or the Bullet

PROJECT 7

THE PADDING OR THE PAVEMENT

Professor Lee, Brother Conrad, graduate students and under-graduate students, friends and enemies: I just can't believe everybody in here is a friend, and I don't want to leave anybody out. The question tonight, as I understand it, is "The Cardinal Revolt, and Should We Wear Helmets?" In my little humble way of understanding it, it points toward either the pavement or the padding.

Before we try and explain what is meant by the pavement or the padding, I would like to clarify something concerning myself. I'm still a grad student; I'm a 5th year here. That's my person standing. Just as Brian is a great undergraduate student cyclist who wears a helmet; and Peter is an undergraduate student crusader for helmet use, I myself am a student, not a undergraduate student, but a graduate student, and I believe in action on all fronts by whatever means necessary.

II. CREATIVITY: REFLECTING

Oral Reflection

After finishing your project, review and answer the following questions by yourself or in a team:

- What did you notice about the use of rhetorical devices in famous speeches?
- What did you take away from ventriloquizing your topic onto the structure of a famous speech?
- Which rhetorical device can you see yourself applying in a future presentation or speech?

8 PERFORMING
APPLICATION
INSTRUMENTAL THEME
SONGS FOR THE NEWS

"Music is the universal language of mankind." — Henry Wadsworth Longfellow

SET THE SCENE

In this chapter, students are asked to explore production music for newscasts. Newscast introduction soundtracks reveal, through sound and aural communication, information about the brand of the organization (personality) and even the type of news. The sounds, rhythms, and other designs can convey immediacy, importance, or drama, signaling our need to pay attention. Sounds can also move us to action. News theme songs can be memorable, helping the audience make associations with the news outlet. These uses, of course, prompt questions, such as whether news instrumental theme songs need to be hummable, for example, or memorable in other ways. Do they appeal to specific audiences? How long should they be? What are they supposed to do? Through the exercises in this chapter, students will explore sound in different and rhetorically significant ways.

Figure 1: Audio Booth. Used under Creative Commons license.

CONNECT TO CREATIVITY

Chapter 8 introduces a creative project called "Broadcast News," which asks you to select free sound clips from sites to represent the content, subject, or thesis of a news brief. Students will browse sites for freely downloadable sound clips that represent a "theme song" for popular news broadcasts. These sound clips can help facilitate meaningful connections to creativity and, in the process, reveal new or previously unavailable rhetorical messages.

Figure 2: Music Note. Flickr.

By working on this activity, you will

- **Explore** how sound creates emotion, energy, interest, and empathy in its listeners and audience members.
- **Analyze** applications and uses of sounds within the context of broadcasting.
- **Reflect** on the rhetorical decisions you made in selecting sounds and why.

LEVEL UP

Free Tools

Part of the assignment is to select and analyze theme songs that are common (or not so common) in broadcast journalism. Theme songs collected must be shared and discussed by the class as well, so it needs to be freely accessible on the Internet. Because the process focuses on aurality, songs must be archived using freely available technologies or sites. The following are free tools that you can use:

Sites		
Tool	URL	Description
Freesound	freesound.org/browse/	Free to download and share.
Free Sound Effects	soundbible.com/free-sound-effects-1.html	Free site for downloading sound effects.
ZapSplat	www.zapsplat.com	Royalty free sound download site.
Ocenaudio.com	www.ocenaudio.com/en/startpage	Free downloadable audio editor.
Hya-wave	hya.io/wave/	Free online audio editor (recommended).

Mobile Applications		
App	URL	Description
Music Maker JAM	https://apple.co/3rnCp2P	Free mobile app that allows you to create, remix, and share sound files.
WavePad	https://apple.co/3NM88SB	Allows you to easily edit and create new music on your device.
DJ Mixer - edjing Mix	https://apple.co/46L55CL	Allows you to make songs and music.

Learn More

You'll find more clips and other examples of aural communication than you can imagine on the web. Many sites and sources offer high-quality, freely available sounds ready for download or use in a variety of applications. Some, however, are not as reliable and should be carefully vetted. We've distilled sites options into several examples for you as you begin your exploration into this project.

Begin by exploring the example of news sounds clips provided by https://soundbible.com/tags-news.html as a start. Sounds are throughout the news and prevalent in our daily lives. Then, access the samples provided below:

"The Importance of Music in Advertising and Branding": https://bit.ly/designforcomposition81

NBC Nightly News Theme Song: https://bit.ly/designforcomposition-nbc

Fox News Channel Theme Song: https://bit.ly/designforcomposition-fox

CNN World News Theme Song: https://bit.ly/designforcomposition-cnn

CNN Breaking News Theme Song: https://bit.ly/designforcomposition-cnnbreaking

PBS News Hour Theme Song (2015): https://bit.ly/designforcomposition-newshour

PBS All Things Considered Theme Song: https://bit.ly/designforcomposition-allthings

CREATIVE PROJECT

Broadcast News

BEFORE YOU BEGIN

Before you begin with the project, listen to sounds from https://www.storyblocks.com/audio/search/broadcast-news-audio. How do these sounds affect your understanding of content available via the news? What meanings or interpretations can you make from these sounds? How might audiences interpret them in different contexts?

Group Activity: Up to three participants.

Total Estimated Time: 1.5 hours for Doing and Reflecting.

Skills: Application of creativity through sound and audio, understanding of aural communication (often use and applications of sounds) and its impact on audience meaning.

(Optional) Sharing: Your instructors may wish you to share your recording online through Tumblr, Wordpress, or your course management system.

I. CREATIVITY: DOING

Overview

This exercise has two parts: Explore and Create. First you will practice analyzing sounds and news broadcast introduction soundtracks to identify prevailing ideas or concepts projected through news brief theme songs. You will then create your own news broadcast introduction soundtrack from among a set of freely available sound clips. The goal of this project is to explore the role of music and sound(s) (aural communication) in communicating to an audience.

CHAPTER EIGHT: BROADCAST NEWS

Directions for Exploring

(Approx. 30 minutes)

1. **Listen** to the old and new versions of the NPR introduction theme, available here: https://www.nytimes.com/2019/05/05/business/media/npr-morning-edition-theme-song.html. What differences do you notice?

2. **Review** the reactions to the revised Morning Edition NPR soundtrack: https://n.pr/3pKUqrb.

3. **Consider** the reactions to the revised soundtrack. Do you have similar reactions or feelings? Are there soundtracks that have been memorable for you?

4. **Discuss** soundtracks that have been memorable. What makes them memorable? What memories do you have?

Directions for Creating

(Approx. 45 minutes)

1. **Create** your own news soundtrack introduction (or "theme song") using the freely available online audio editing tools and mobile applications provided earlier in this chapter.

2. **Identify** your audience: who is it for?

3. **Identify** your news: what kind of news is it?

4. **Mix or modify** sounds in creative ways for your newscast that are unique to you and represent an introduction that you would have for your own news show.

5. **Recall** the qualities that made the samples provided in this chapter unique and memorable.

Your news soundtrack theme song should convey timeliness, importance, intrigue, immediacy, and other qualities that command our attention when listening to breaking news on television networks. Your goal is to convey meaning, a message, through sound, using at least the tools above.

PROJECT 8

II. CREATIVITY: REFLECTING

Oral Reflection: Discussion

(Approx. 15 minutes)

Depending on how much time there is in class, instructors may ask you to provide oral or written reflection. The following are questions you can ask your peer(s):

- What elements of the news broadcast news theme song samples stood out for you?
- Why did you choose to create your news broadcast theme song the way you did?
- How did you design it for your specific audience? For your specific type of news?
- How long is it? Why might that be the case?
- How does the news broadcast theme song do what it does?
- How did speed, rhythm, or tone influence your decision?

9 COMPOSING PRODUCTION
MAKING YOUR OWN PORTMANTEAU

"'Twas brillig, and the slithy toves
    Did gyre and gimble in the wabe:
All mimsy were the borogoves,
    And the mome raths outgrabe.

Beware the Jabberwock, my son!
    The jaws that bite, the claws that catch!
Beware the Jubjub bird, and shun
    The frumious Bandersnatch!"

— Lewis Caroll, "Jabberwocky"

SET THE SCENE

The combination of words is called portmanteau: "two meanings packed up into one word," as Humpty Dumpty notes in Lewis Carroll's *Through the Looking Glass*. One of the most memorable portmanteau poems in English, Caroll's "Jabberwocky" is also considered a "nonsense" poem. Its playful combination of sound features suggests images and ideas that closely approximate actual words we know. For instance, "brillig" sounds like a combination of "brilliant" and "big."

Figure 1: Illustration of the Jabberwocky from Lewis Carroll's *Through the Looking Glass and What Alice Found There* (1871).

Other examples of portmanteau in Carroll's book include the "Bread and Butter-Fly," which combines "bread and butter" with "fly" to humorous effect. Portmanteau words work best when they clearly hint at words that readers might recognize or associate with something in particular. And while portmanteau words may seem like schoolyard fun, creativity skills needed to make "new words" based on association of sounds from familiar words are valuable: some people make a living as "naming experts," coming up with new names for startup companies and products. Real companies like "Ideo" (global design company"), "Bankity" (digital banking app), "Fintual" (financial management platform), "Goodr" (food management platform that donates excess food to charities) are examples of names that recall one or more familiar words; companies hope that the ideas associated with these "word-sounds" will rub onto the brand. Portmanteau words are also frequently generated in media, such as murse (man + purse) bromance (brother + romance, close friendship), mansplaining (man explaining to women), and Brexit (Britain + exiting EU).

CONNECT TO CREATIVITY

In this exercise, you will explore the suggestiveness of sound and meaning in spoken word by creating new words that combine the sounds (and meaning) of two "old" ones. More specifically, you'll be creating a new portmanteau word to explore a popular behavior, activity, or phenomenon at your learning institution or community. By joining two or three speech sounds to invent words, you can improve your own awareness of sound in actual words used to evoke ideas, associations, and emotion.

www.fromoldbooks.org

Figure 2: Illustration of Bread and Butterfly from Lewis Caroll's *Through the Looking Glass and What Alice Found There* (1871).

By working on this activity, you will

- **Apply divergent thinking** by generating many words associated with a particular idea.
- **Creatively combine** two or more syllables/sounds from each word to generate a new word.
- **Reflect** on your choices and the choices of others by sharing.

LEVEL UP

Free Tools

To help your Creative Project, we've assembled two free sites. Use these sites as a starting point for this project.

Sites		
Tool	URL	Description
Google Drive Document	https://www.google.com/drive/	Google Drive is a synchronous, collaborative slide-design platform. It allows you to create shareable documents.
VoiceThread	https://voicethread.com/	VoiceThread is a cloud-based multimedia application that allows you to upload, share, and discuss documents, presentations, images, audio files and videos. You can register for a free account that allows you to create up to five VoiceThreads.

CREATIVE PROJECT

Make Your Own Portmanteau

BEFORE YOU BEGIN

Group Activity: Up to three participants.

Total Estimated Time: 1 hour for Doing and Reflecting.

Skills: Application of creativity through divergent and convergent thinking.

Sharing Options: Depending on how your class or group is asked to deliver this project, you may be sharing the work virtually or in person. We suggest sharing your new words using Google Drive document or another platform that your instructor identifies.

Synchronous/Asynchronous: This activity can be conducted both synchronously and asynchronously with some modification.

For live activity (in person or synchronous), we recommend that you work with a group to analyze new words in your Google Drive document or another platform that your instructor identifies.

For asynchronous interactions with your class or group, share your method using VoiceThread. Please refer to the steps under Creativity: Doing.

I. CREATIVITY: DOING

*"Door: Why it's simply impassible!
Alice: Why, don't you mean impossible?
Door: No, I do mean impassible. (chuckles) Nothing's impossible!"*

— *Lewis Carroll, Through the Looking Glass and What Alice Found There (1871)*

Directions for Live (In-Person) Activity

Modeling (10 mins.)

1. Discuss the sample provided and the parts in the quote opening this section of the chapter.

2. Think about: What are the two words that make the portmanteau word "impassible"? How is it appropriate in the given situation of the story?

Practice (30 mins.)

Using the Portmanteau Generator provided below this table, complete these two steps:

Step 1: Divergent thinking

1. Think about an action, activity, phenomenon that happens at your institution, community, or work environment.

2. Identify two words that might help define that action, activity or phenomenon.

3. Fill out Column #1 and #2 with words that are synonyms to the two words that you've generated. Try to fill at least three boxes in each column.

Step 2: Convergent thinking

1. Create at least three variations of your portmanteau word. At least one should experiment with sound (sound like a word but not necessarily follow the original spelling).

2. Choose the final word either from Part 2 or a version of the words in Part 2.

3. Write out the justification of your choice.

Share (20 mins.)

1. Share your answer on the portmanteau generator.

2. You (or your team) should identify: A) original words/ideas, B) selection process and how you brainstormed your words, C) how you generated three different versions of the portmanteau word and your final selection.

Modeling (10 mins.)

1. Discuss the sample provided and the parts in the quote opening this section of the chapter.

2. Think about: What are the two words that make the portmanteau word "impassible"? How is it appropriate in the given situation of the story?

3. Record the discussion via video and post to your class discussion board.

Practice (30 mins.)

Using the Portmanteau Generator provided below this table, complete these two steps:

Step 1: Divergent thinking

1. Think about an action, activity, phenomenon that happens at your institution, community, or work environment.

2. Identify two words that might help define that action, activity or phenomenon.

3. Fill out columns #1 and #2 with words that are synonyms to the two words that you've generated using a Google Drive document. Try to fill at least three boxes in each column.

Step 2: Convergent thinking

1. Create at least three variations of your portmanteau word. At least one should experiment with sound (sound like a word but not necessarily follow the original spelling).

2. Choose the final word either from Part 2 or a version of the words in Part 2.

3. Write out the justification of your choice in your Google Drive document Portmanteau Generator.

Share

1. Record your explanation using VoiceThread.

2. Share the link to your VoiceThread with your peers.

Sample Portmanteau Generator

Part One: Divergent Thinking (15 mins.)

Divergent thinking: coming up with as many words as possible connected to your idea.

Fill in the columns with as many words as possible.

Idea: Someone who walks around campus while constantly using their phones

Word Column 1	Word Column 2
Cellphone	Walker
Smartphone	Ambler
Cell	Zombie
Phone	Schlepper
Mobile	Shuffler
	Passer

Part Two: Convergent Thinking (10 mins.)

Convergent thinking: generating many variations with the original version to come up with something new or original.

Portmanteau Version 1	Phonezombie
Portmanteau Version 2	Mobilezomb
Portmanteau Version 3 (Sound Variation)	Mobezombie

Part Three: Your Portmanteau (5 mins.)

Final Word	Mobezomb
Explanation	Easy to say the sounds together. Two syllables are easier to say than three. Can't cut cut out too much of zombie—otherwise you couldn't recognize it. Cut enough from the word "mobile," so that you can hear the first syllable that is part of "mobile" (mobe not mob).

Your Portmanteau Generator

Part One: Divergent Thinking
Fill in the columns with as many words as possible.

Idea: Someone who walks around campus while constantly using their phones

Word Column 1	Word Column 2

Part Two: Convergent Thinking 10 mins.)
Convergent thinking: generating many variations with the original version to come up with something new or original.

Portmanteau Version 1	
Portmanteau Version 2	
Portmanteau Version 3 (Sound Variation)	

Part Three: Your Portmanteau (5 mins.)

Final Word	
Explanation	.

II. CREATIVITY: REFLECTING

Oral Reflection

Now that you've finished your project, take a moment to reflect on what you learned. Answer the following questions individually or as a team:

Questions about Divergent Thinking

- How difficult was it for you to come up with two words communicating the idea/concept of the portmanteau?
- Did you find that you discover words that you didn't expect?

Questions about Convergent Thinking

- How challenging was it to generate three versions of the portmanteau word?
- How did this process help you select the final word?

10 SEEING PRODUCTION ALBUM ART AND DISCOVERING TYPOGRAPHY

"I learned about serif and sans serif typefaces, about varying the amount of space between different letter combinations, about what makes great typography great. . . . None of this had even a hope of any practical application in my life. But ten years later, when we were designing the first Macintosh computer, it all came back to me. And we designed it all into the Mac." — Steve Jobs

SET THE SCENE

In his commencement speech at Stanford University on June 12, 2005, Steve Jobs does not describe the first Macintosh computer in terms of its unique graphical user interface or its successful adoption of computer mouse technology. Rather, Jobs focused on the Macintosh's ability to produce "beautiful typography." As a result of the Mac's application of typography, Simon Garfield, author of *Just My Type*, writes, "Computers have rendered us all gods of type."

Figure 1: John Ray, "T" Woodcut. From oldbooks.org.

Woodcut typography as a communication application is ancient. In the nineteenth and twentieth century, modern typography was related to advertising and other promotional formats such as signage, posters, book covers, logos, and packaging.

Figure 2: Santiago Orange Growers Association. Advertisement for Searchlight brand oranges. Orange Public Library. Orange, California.

Typography involves the arrangement of type through selection of typeface, point size, and other features that form a language. "Typeface" refers specifically to the design of a collection or set of one or more fonts, such as Times New Roman, Helvetica, and Garamond.

Times New Roman
Helvetica
Garamond

Figure 3: Three fonts created in Microsoft Word: Times New Roman, Helvetica, and Garamond.

"Font" now refers to the set of computer files associated with the typeface. Since the computer allows us to adjust the type by bold, italics, underline styles, independent of the typeface, font and typeface are often used interchangeably.

CONNECT TO CREATIVITY

Chapter 10 introduces a multisensory creative project called "Album Art," which asks you, with a group of your peers, to apply creativity as exploration through typeface and graphic design. More specifically, by connecting sound and lyrics in songs with visual elements in typeface, you will learn how typefaces carry personalities, emotion, and feeling. Furthermore, you'll discover how layout and color can add more meaning to the visual design message you wish to create.

10

Figure 4: Two versions of album art using the title of Mark Ronson's song "Uptown Funk."

By working on this activity, you will

- **Explore** how typeface carries distinct "personality" profiles or attributes.
- **Translate** concepts from one modality (sound) to another (visual).
- **Create** an album cover with typeface, layout, and color.
- **Reflect** on your creative choices in typeface and design.

LEVEL UP

Free Tools

Designers can find hundreds of freely available tools on the web. We've assembled some of the top free sites for you here. Use these sites as a starting point to identify fonts for use in this design project.

Tool	URL	Description
Dafont.com	www.dafont.com	Over thirty thousand font families. Download and install to use on Microsoft Word and PowerPoint. Many are free.
Google Fonts	fonts.google.com	Hundreds of free and open-source font families that you can add to your Google Doc and Google Slides. Use filters to view categories of typefaces.
Adobe Color CC	https://color.adobe.com/create/color-wheel	This tool helps you select color themes through preset color rules or create your own palette of colors. Start with selecting one color and go from there.

Learn More

You'll find more design perspectives than you could ever wish for available freely on the web. Many of these sources offer good advice based on experience and even, at times, research. Some of them are not as reliable. We've distilled these sites into some of the best available for you as you begin your design work. You might find the samples and perspectives on the following page inspiring.

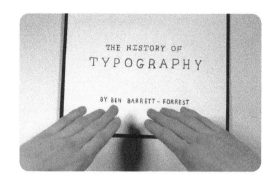

Ben Barrett-Forrest, "The History of Typography," Vimeo, 5 min., accessed 11 May 2016, https://vimeo.com/65353988. Barrett-Forrest provides a creative paper-letter animation that documents the history of typography.

Helvetica, **directed by Gary Hustwit, Documentary Film, Plexifilm, 2007.** This documentary film explores the development of typeface and graphic design through the story of Helvetica. It includes interesting and engaging discussions about typeface design by famous graphic and typeface designers. Rent for less than an App on Amazon. You can also purchase on Amazon and iTunes.

Simon Garfield, *Just My Type*, **Gotham Books, 2011.** This international bestseller is easy to read and provides an exciting backstory to the history of typography. It includes font examples, history, and background along with samples that help readers establish context for font uses.

CREATIVE PROJECT

Album Art by Typography

BEFORE YOU BEGIN

Watch Ben Barret-Forrest's "The History of Typography" or Gary Hustwit's *Helvetica* to better understand the personality of type and how it is used in the real world.

Group Activity: Up to three participants.

Total Estimated Time: 1.5 hours for Doing and Reflecting.

Skills: Discovery process, typographical awareness, visual design application.

Sharing Options: Depending on how your class or group is asked to deliver this project, you may be sharing the work virtually or in person. We suggest sharing your album art cover using Google Drive or another platform that your instructor identifies.

Synchronous/Asynchronous: This activity can be conducted both synchronously and asynchronously with some modification.

For live activity (in person or synchronous), we recommend that you work with a group to analyze typography in your Google Drive document or another platform that your instructor identifies.

For asynchronous interactions with your class or group, share your album cover via Google Drive. Please refer to the steps under Creativity: Doing.

I. CREATIVITY: DOING

"It is the designer/typgographer's task to match form with content." — Nick Shinn

Overview

Creatively design an album cover only using typeface and graphic design. In this challenge, you'll explore an important aspect of creativity —experimenting and discovering —by translating something from one mode into another. In this case, you'll take a favorite song (sound and/or lyrics) and visualize it in type.

Directions

1. Choose a title of a song by a specific artist.
2. Turn the title (and the artist's name) into album art using written text only.

Steps for Live (In-Person) Activity	
Select	**Select** a song to share with your group and listen to it.
List	**List** three attributes (describe song with three adjectives or cultural associations).
Select	**Select** custom font.
Design	**Design** album cover using only font, color, and layout choices.

Steps for Asynchronous Activity	
Select	**Select** a song to share with your group and listen to it.
List	**List** three attributes (describe song with three adjectives or cultural associations) using a Google Drive document.
Select	**Select** custom font.
Design	**Design** album cover using only font, color, and layout choices with one of the freely available tools provided in this chapter. Post to Google Drive or another platform your instructor identifies.

It's very important to define the attributes of the song before selecting the font that best represents the music (try using the table provided in the next section). You will then be able to narrow your font choices by visiting font libraries available at **DaFont.com** and **Google Font** (see "Free Tools" for more details). You can also draw your font by hand. Finally, when designing the album cover, you should consider color and graphic effects (such as the size of the fonts, transparency, and color of fonts or the background) to help you convey the message, tone, emotion, quality, or artist's ethos. **Adobe Color CC** is a free tool that can help you use colors effectively. Be prepared to speak about how typeface and graphic design relays your "message" about the song.

PROJECT 10

Your Album Cover	
Name of Song: **Composer/Singer:**	
Song Attributes	
Consider (1) sounds, pacing, rhythm; (2) use of instruments, singer's voice (sad, happy, energetic, etc.); (3) how the song and its sounds make you feel; (4) Meaning of lyrics (if any)	
1	
2	
3	

Tips: How to Creatively Select the Type

Personality choices. What kind of personality do you want the music to project? Use the attributes you've written in the table above to help you narrow the choice of fonts to two or three.

Meaning choices. In what way do you want information or tone from your song to be carried through type (your font choice) and by type (by words themselves)?

Legibility choices. Should the type be readable? Do you want the type to be looked at more than read? What is the effect of being legible or not for your type?

Graphic design choices. How do you want the visual design choices of the entire album to impact the "feeling" or "message" delivered by the type? For instance how will color, placement, spacing between letters or words (called kerning), angle, or transparency impact the meaning of your album message?

Student Samples

Example 1: Miles Davis, "So What."
Attributes: Slow tempo, relaxed feel, rough sound.

Example 2: Miley Cyrus, "Party in the USA."
Attributes: Spunky, free-spirited, youthful.

PROJECT 10

II. CREATIVITY: REFLECTING

Oral Reflection: Peer Feedback

Provide feedback by exchanging the album art between teams. Listen carefully to the response without interruption and take notes. The following are questions you can ask your team members.

Test typographic impact

- When you look at my choice of typography, what one or two adjectives come to mind?
- Share your thoughts about the attributes you hoped to convey.

Test focus

- Where are the focus points for you on this album?
- Share your strategy for design.

Test color and design

- Is the color effectively used to unify the different parts of the album?
- What other ways might I use color or graphic effectively to more clearly convey the message?

Report back

- At the end of the oral reflection session, report on the feedback that you received and your own experience working on the project.
- What did you discover about typeface?

Written Reflection: Individual Response

Write a paragraph in response to the following questions. Support your ideas by providing concrete references to your experience in the exercise:

- What did you enjoy most about designing your album art?
- What was the most challenging?
- If you had more time, what would you do to enhance creativity in your album art?
- What creative role did typeface have for your album art?
- What creative role did other graphic effects such as layout and color have for your album art?

11

PERFORMING
PRODUCTION
CONTACT
[OBJECT]
IMPROVISATION

"Each party of the duet freely improvises with an aim to working along the easiest pathways available to their mutually moving masses." — Steve Paxton

SET THE SCENE

Contact improvisation is a dance form, often used as an exercise, to help dancers explore and enhance awareness of the body's range of movement through space in response to gravity, momentum, and the dancer's partner. First introduced by Steve Paxton, contact improvisation is, as the name suggests, experimental "improvisation": it emphasizes letting the body movement happen through reflexive action —not, as one dance instructor notes, "doing whatever you want." Secondly, the dancer works to explore the "center" of movement with a partner, with whom s/he is always touching through rolls, lifts, movement, and stretching. The goal of these movements is to broaden our sense of physicality in movement and become more sensitive to touch —ultimately, discovering your own movement possibilities and patterns. The aim of these explorations is to increase your awareness and connection with body movement and your own body's "voice."

Figure 1: Dancing figures

CONNECT TO CREATIVITY

Chapter 11 introduces a performative creative project called "Contact [Object] improvisation." Instead of working with a physical partner, you will apply contact improvisation with an object of your choice. More specifically, by connecting your body with an object, you will explore rolls, lifts, stretches, and other movements with the object. The contact [object] improvisation includes specific activities (e.g. weight transfer through rolls, lifts, falls, stretches) in a space where legs and arms can move, if possible. You will be asked to reflect on your experience with contact improvisation as it relates to body movement, touch, and space.

Figure 2: Green and white cube.

By working on this activity, you will

- **Explore** new body movement possibilities.
- **Increase** awareness of one's own physicality and movement.
- **Reflect** on your creative movements and your own body voice, connect with oral communication.

LEVEL UP

Free Tools

Tool	URL	Description
VoiceThread A multimodal platform that can be used on any computer or device	voicethread.com	VoiceThread is a cloud-based multimedia application that allows you to upload, share,and discuss documents, presentations, images, audio files and videos. You can register for a free account that allows you to create up to five VoiceThreads.

Learn More

Steve Paxton, "Contact Improvisation," *The Drama Review: TDR*. vol. 19, no. 1. **Post-modern dance issue (March 1975): 40-42.** This article presents the theory behind contact improvisation.

"Contact Improvisation—A Couple of Basic Exercises" YouTube. https://bit.ly/designforcomposition111. This video presents contact improvisation as dance exercises —both single and with a partner. It illustrates the way touch, weight, momentum, balance, flow play a role in shaping movement. Students can use this video to understand the kind of movements they may want to explore with their object.

Dryden, Nathan. "We Rise and Fall Together. Contact Improv." TEDx. YouTube. October 31, 2017. https://bit.ly/designforcomposition112. This TEDx video demonstrates contact improvisation as a dance form, illustrating spontaneous movement in physical contact. Here the dance is preceded by a statement that is then communicated or voiced through contact improvisation. This video can help students get a better sense of how the body can have a "voice" through movement.

CREATIVE PROJECT

Performance Exploration: Contact [Object] Improvisation

BEFORE YOU BEGIN

Watch one of the videos listed in *Learn More*.

Group Activity: Up to three participants.

Total Estimated Time: 1.5 hours for Doing and Reflecting.

Skills: Discover process, body awareness and exploration, touch awareness.

Sharing Options: Depending on how your class or group is asked to deliver this project, you may be sharing the work virtually or in person. You may be asked to share your video response to the form through VoiceThread, YouTube, or other platforms that allow for video sharing.

I. CREATIVITY: DOING

"Everything in the universe has rhythm. Everything dances." — Maya Angelou

Overview

Creatively explore contact improvisation using an object as your partner. In this challenge, you'll explore an important aspect of creativity —spontaneity —by allowing your body to balance, weigh, roll, and flow with an object that it is continually in contact with for 30 seconds.

Directions for Live (In-Person) Activity

1. **Watch** one of the videos (exercise or TEDx) listed under *Learn More*; fill out the contact [object] improvisation form, part 1 (see below).

2. **Select** an object (it can be something you can hold, or something you can touch like furniture). Do not choose anything sharp or something that can break. List that object under part 2 of the form.

3. **Find a place/space** where you can move. This can be a room if it has enough space for movement. It can also be outside at a park, backyard, patio, etc. Answer part 3 of the form (describe place/space). Review the list of three attributes that you wrote in the form and attempt to include them in your own contact improvisation.

4. **Time your contact improvisation** (start to finish).

5. **Answer reflection questions in part 4.**

6. **VoiceThread or other platforms:** On VoiceThread you can upload your form and talk through each of the four parts of the form, explaining the attributes you initially observed, object you used, place and time you recorded, and your answers to the reflection questions. Alternatively, you can record your responses as a video and upload to YouTube.

7. **Share:** Be prepared to share the response.

Contact [Object] Improvisation Form

Part One: Video Observation

Attributes observed in contact improvisation

Identify three key attributes that you noticed about contact improvisation in the video. List your observations below.

Some common attributes are:
- constant contact (never losing touch with the partner or object)
- constant movement
- movement flowing/responding to its own weight/gravity or the weight of the object/partner
- movement that is not planned (spontaneous)
- movement in response to touch
- transitions of the body from one shape or form or another through rolls, turns, flow

1

2

3

Part Two: Contact Object

Contact Object	Description of your contact object. (Show the object when you are on VoiceThread!)

Practice contact improvisation.
Time yourself for 3 minutes (minimum).
Apply each of the three attributes listed in Part 1, one minute at a time.
Try to be present and aware of the movements you make.

Place/space	
Time started	
Time ended	

When you practiced contact improvisation with attributes (listed in Part 1), which attribute was the most interesting to apply? **Which was the most difficult?**	
How would you describe your experience with applying one of the attributes in contact improvisation?	
What kind of creative awareness did you experience during this activity? **How might this awareness help you when you think about oral communication, use of gestures or body, use of props in presentations or the presentation space?**	

INDEX

ABOUT THE AUTHORS

Sohui Lee is Associate Professor and Faculty Director of the Writing and Multiliteracy Center at California State University Channel Islands (CSUCI). She received a BA in English from UCLA and MA and PhD in English from Boston University. She was awarded a postdoctoral fellowship at Stanford University and then taught college writing in the Program of Writing and Rhetoric while working as Assistant and Associate Director of Stanford's Hume Center of Writing and Speaking. At CSUCI, she founded the Writing and Multiliteracy Center. Her research scholarship includes multiliteracy pedagogy, multimodal communication, and academic creativity. She is co-editor of *The Routledge Reader on Writing Centers and New Media* (2013) and *Disruptive Stories: Amplifying Voices from Writing Center Margins* (Utah State University Press, forthcoming 2024). She also worked as associate editor at *WLN: A Journal of Writing Center Scholarship* (2017–2021) and has published over thirty articles and chapters in peer-reviewed journals such as *Writing Center Journal, WLN, Praxis, Southern Discourse in the Center, American Periodicals, Across the Disciplines*, and *Computers and Composition.*

Russell Carpenter is Assistant Provost and Professor of English at Eastern Kentucky University. Carpenter serves as editor-in-chief of the *Journal of Faculty Development* and past editor of the *Communication Center Journal.* Carpenter has written or edited a wide range of books, including *Engaging Millennial Faculty, Studio-Based Approaches for Multimodal Projects, Writing Studio Pedagogy*, and *Sustainable Learning Spaces.* Articles have appeared in *Computers and Composition, Journal of Learning Spaces, Across the Disciplines, Journal of Excellence in College Teaching*, and the *Journal of Creative and Artistic Education*, among others. Carpenter is the former president of the Southeastern Writing Center Association and chair of the National Association of Communication Centers. He received the 2018 Turner Award from the National Association of Communication Centers, along with the 2015 Preston Award for Leadership. In 2020, he was awarded the Southeastern Writing Center Association's highest recognition, the Achievement Award. Carpenter has received multiple top-panel awards from the National Communication Association's Communication Center division for scholarship focused on innovations in multimodal communication, program design, and communication-focused partnerships.